KEYNOTES FOR PILOTS

KEYFACTS for
EASA PART-FCL PPL
Examinations 2015

010 AIR LAW AND ATC PROCEDURES
020 AIRCRAFT GENERAL KNOWLEDGE
030 FLIGHT PERFORMANCE AND PLANNING
040 HUMAN PERFORMANCE AND LIMITATIONS
050 METEOROLOGY
060 NAVIGATION
070 OPERATIONAL PROCEDURES
080 PRINCIPLES OF FLIGHT
090 COMMUNICATIONS

GW00579993

Dr. Stuart E. Smith
Published by Cranfield Aviation Training School Ltd.

KEYNOTES FOR PILOTS

KEYFACTS for EASA PART-FCL PPL examinations

British Library Cataloguing in Publication Data.
A catalogue record for this book is available from the British Library.

This edition:
ISBN 978-1-907782-18-3

Previous editions:
ISBN 0-9540275-5-8 (1st edition, 2002)
ISBN 978-1-907782-13-8 (2nd edition, 2004)

Further volumes in this series are:
Keynotes for Pilots KEYFACTS for EASA PART-FCL ATPL examinations Vol. 1 (ISBN 978-1-907782-15-2)
Keynotes for Pilots KEYFACTS for EASA PART-FCL ATPL examinations Vol. 2 (ISBN 978-1-907782-16-9)
Keynotes for Pilots KEYFACTS for EASA PART-FCL ATPL examinations Vol. 3 (ISBN 978-1-907782-17-6)
Key Facts Maths & Physics for Pilots (ISBN 978-1-907782-14-5)

and further publications by Keynotes Aviation Ltd. are:
Vol 1: The JAA CPL (A) Skill Test (ISBN 0-9540275-0-7)
Vol 2: The JAA Instrument Rating (A) Skill Test (ISBN 0-9540275-1-5)
Vol 3: Multi-Crew Co-operation (ISBN 0-9540275-4-X)

Dr. Stuart E. Smith
Published by Cranfield Aviation Training School Ltd.

FOREWORD

Dr. Stuart E. Smith has an acknowledged academic background and trained for his Commercial Pilot Licence (CPL) and Instrument Rating at Oxford, UK. He is currently Head of Training at Cranfield Aviation Training School (a school specialising in Theoretical Knowledge Training for Private, Commercial and Airline Pilots) and is a Private and Commercial Flight Instructor, a Flight Instructor Course Instructor and a PPL Theoretical Knowledge Examiner at Cranfield.

Dr. Stuart E. Smith has collated his extensive experience to provide you with this essential guide to the EASA PART-FCL PPL and the examinations.

The Keynotes style with alternating pages of text and space for your personal keynotes relevant to your ground school will ensure that this volume will become a valuable aid to your theoretical knowledge training.

CONTENTS

INTRODUCTION

When using this book remember that the key to obtaining a first time pass at EASA PART-FCL examinations is good preparation and quality instruction. The EASA PART-FCL ground examinations provide a fundamental platform in your education as a pilot for the PART-FCL PPL (and the PART-FCL LAPL). Do not underestimate the work that you will involve yourself in to pass the examinations. It is important to condense and reduce your notes into quick easy reference Key Facts and if at all possible make your own personal version since you will understand your own writings better.

In the U.K. a National Private Pilots Licence (NPPL) exists. The theoretical knowledge examinations for this licence are the same theoretical knowledge examinations, which are used for the EASA PART-FCL PPL and LAPL. This book therefore serves to prepare students for the U.K. National PPL, the PART-FCL PPL and the PART-FCL LAPL.

This book is unique and employs a question - answer; challenge - response style of text. This will enable you to question yourself, and enable even a person untrained in the subject to question you, to assist your retention of Key Facts.

This volume should be read in full to prepare you for your examinations and each section can be used to assist you in preparation for each examination. On test day if you have prepared well enough you will not need it.

NEW SYLLABUS EASA PART-FCL EXAMINATIONS

The new syllabus PART-FCL PPL (A) was introduced on the 1st September 2013. From that date all old syllabus PPL (A) examinations were withdrawn. Candidates who had already commenced an examination series (sat one or more examinations) under the old syllabus, but had not completed all the required examinations for Licence issue before 1st September 2013, have to complete any outstanding examinations to the new syllabus standard. In the case of Flight Performance and Planning (FPP) and Navigation, a student had to pass both subjects prior to 1st September 2013 if examined to the old syllabus; no credit is given for a pass in one subject only. If under such circumstances a re-sit is required then it will be considered as a first attempt (of four) in those subjects only.

COMPOSITION OF THE EASA PART-FCL EXAMINATIONS

There are 9 PPL(A) written examinations. Each question in each examination paper is followed by several alternative answers; in other words questions are multiple choice and offer 4 possible answers: A, B, C, or D. Each examination offers a total mark out of 100. The pass mark for each examination is 75%. No credit or penalty is given for unanswered or incorrect answers to questions.

Key Facts for these examinations are covered in one volume of this series.

PASS RULES FOR THE EASA PART-FCL EXAMINATIONS

An applicant will have been deemed to have successfully completed the required theoretical knowledge examinations for the PPL (A) when he / she has passed all of the required examination papers within a period of 18 months counted from the end of the calendar month when the applicant first attempted an examination.

If an applicant fails to pass one of the examination papers within four attempts, or has failed to pass all papers within six sittings or a period of 18 months, he / she shall have to re-take the complete of examination papers.

A sitting for a PPL is defined as the attendance at an examination centre for the purpose of taking one or more examinations. When taking more than one examination, these must be completed in a maximum of ten consecutive days. Only one attempt at each paper may be made in any one sitting. A candidate is not compelled to wait until the end of the ten consecutive day period before attempting the re-sit of a failed paper, but whenever a re-sit is attempted a further sitting will be considered to have commenced.

VALIDITY PERIOD FOR THE THEORETICAL KNOWLEDGE EXAMINATIONS AND SKILL TEST FOR THE PPL

A pass will be accepted for the grant of a PART-FCL PPL (A) during the 24 months from the actual date of successfully completing all of the theoretical knowledge examinations.

EQUIPMENT USED IN THE EXAMINATIONS

Applicants may use the following equipment in an examination: 1) a scientific, non-programmable, non-alphanumeric calculator without specific aviation functions; 2) mechanical slide rule; 3) protractor; compasses and dividers; 5) ruler. Charts will be provided.

EXAMINATION STRUCTURE

Subject	Number of Questions	Duration
Air Law	16	35 min
Aircraft General Knowledge	16	35 min
Flight Planning and Performance	12	45 min
Meteorology	16	50 min
Human Performance and Limitations	12	25 min
Navigation	12	45 min
Operational Procedures	12	30 min
Principles of Flight	12	35 min
Communications	12	35 min

THE EASA PART-FCL PPL SYLLABUS

The EASA PART-FCL PPL syllabus is the basis for the PPL theoretical study and learning. PPL examination questions are constructed to match the syllabus. The syllabus is included here for reference purposes:

SUBPART C — PRIVATE PILOT LICENCE (PPL), SAILPLANE PILOT LICENCE (SPL) and BALLOON PILOT LICENCE (BPL) AMC1 FCL.210; FCL.215

SYLLABUS OF THEORETICAL KNOWLEDGE FOR THE PPL(A)
The following tables contain the syllabi for the courses of theoretical knowledge, as well as for the theoretical knowledge examinations for the PPL(A) and PPL(H). The training and examination should cover aspects related to non-technical skills in an integrated manner, taking into account the particular risks associated to the licence and the activity. An approved course should comprise at least 100 h of theoretical knowledge instruction. However the UK CAA have absolved schools of the 100 h requirement but the syllabus must still be demonstrated to have been covered. This theoretical knowledge instruction provided by the ATO should include a certain element of formal classroom work but may include also such facilities as interactive video, slide or tape presentation, computer-based training and other

media distance learning courses. The training organisation responsible for the training has to check if all the appropriate elements of the training course of theoretical knowledge instruction have been completed to a satisfactory standard before recommending the applicant for the examination. The applicable items for each licence are marked with 'x'. An 'x' on the main title of a subject means that all the sub-divisions are applicable.

		(A)
1	**AIR LAW AND ATC PROCEDURES**	
	International law: conventions, agreements and organisations	
	The Convention on international civil aviation (Chicago) Doc. 7300/6	
	Part I Air Navigation: relevant parts of the following chapters:	x
	(a) general principles and application of the convention; (b) flight over territory of Contracting States; (c) nationality of aircraft; (d) measures to facilitate air navigation; (e) conditions to be fulfilled on aircraft; (f) international standards and recommended practices; (g) validity of endorsed certificates and licences; (h) notification of differences.	
	Part II The International Civil Aviation Organisation (ICAO): objectives and composition	x
	Annex 8: Airworthiness of aircraft	
	Foreword and definitions	x
	Certificate of airworthiness	x
	Annex 7: Aircraft nationality and registration marks	
	Foreword and definitions	x
	Common- and registration marks	x
	Certificate of registration and aircraft nationality	x
	Annex 1: Personnel licensing	
	Definitions	x
	Relevant parts of Annex 1 connected to Part-FCL and Part-Medical	x
	Annex 2: Rules of the air	
	Essential definitions, applicability of the rules of the air, general rules (except water operations), visual flight rules, signals and interception of civil aircraft	x
	Procedures for air navigation: aircraft operations doc. 8168-ops/611, volume 1	
	Altimeter setting procedures (including IACO doc. 7030 – regional supplementary procedures)	
	Basic requirements (except tables), procedures applicable to operators and pilots (except tables)	x
	Secondary surveillance radar transponder operating procedures (including ICAO Doc. 7030 – regional supplementary procedures)	
	Operation of transponders	x
	Phraseology	x
	Annex 11: Doc. 4444 air traffic management	
	Definitions	x
	General provisions for air traffic services	x
	Visual separation in the vicinity of aerodromes	x
	Procedures for aerodrome control services	x
	Radar services	x

	Flight information service and alerting service		x
	Phraseologies		x
	Procedures related to emergencies, communication failure and contingencies		x
	Annex 15: Aeronautical information service		
	Introduction, essential definitions		x
	AIP, NOTAM, AIRAC and AIC		x
	Annex 14, volume 1 and 2: Aerodromes		
	Definitions		x
	Aerodrome data: conditions of the movement area and related facilities		x
	Visual aids for navigation: (a) indicators and signaling devices; (b) markings; (c) lights; (d) signs; (e) markers.		x
	Visual aids for denoting obstacles: (a) marking of objects; (b) lighting of objects.		x
	Visual aids for denoting restricted use of areas		x
	Emergency and other services: (a) rescue and fire fighting; (b) apron management service.		x
	Annex 12: Search and rescue		
	Essential definitions		x
	Operating procedures: (a) procedures for PIC at the scene of an accident; (b) procedures for PIC intercepting a distress transmission; (c) search and rescue signals.		x
	Search and rescue signals: (a) signals with surface craft; (b) ground or air visual signal code; (c) air or ground signals.		x
	Annex 17: Security		
	General: aims and objectives		x
	Annex 13: Aircraft accident investigation		
	Essential definitions		x
	Applicability		x
	National law		
	National law and differences to relevant ICAO Annexes and relevant EU regulations.		x
2	**HUMAN PERFORMANCE**		
	Human factors: basic concepts		
	Human factors in aviation		
	Becoming a competent pilot		x
	Basic aviation physiology and health maintenance		
	The atmosphere: (a) composition; (b) gas laws.		x
	Respiratory and circulatory systems: (a) oxygen requirement of tissues; (b) functional anatomy; (c) main forms of hypoxia (hypoxic and anaemic): (1) sources, effects and counter-measures of carbon monoxide; (2) counter measures and hypoxia;		x

(3) symptoms of hypoxia. (d) hyperventilation; (e) the effects of accelerations on the circulatory system; (f) hypertension and coronary heart disease.		
Man and environment		
Central, peripheral and autonomic nervous systems	x	
Vision: (a) functional anatomy; (b) visual field, foveal and peripheral vision; (c) binocular and monocular vision; (d) monocular vision cues; (e) night vision; (f) visual scanning and detection techniques and importance of 'look-out'; (g) defective vision.		
Hearing: (a) descriptive and functional anatomy; (b) flight related hazards to hearing; (c) hearing loss.	x	
Equilibrium: (a) functional anatomy; (b) motion and acceleration; (c) motion sickness.	x	
Integration of sensory inputs: (a) spatial disorientation: forms, recognition and avoidance;	x	
(b) illusions: forms, recognition and avoidance: (1) physical origin; (2) physiological origin; (3) psychological origin. (c) approach and landing problems.		
Health and hygiene		
Personal hygiene: personal fitness	x	
Body rhythm and sleep: (a) rhythm disturbances; (b) symptoms, effects and management.	x	
Problem areas for pilots: (a) common minor ailments including cold, influenza and gastro-intestinal upset; (b) entrapped gases and barotrauma, (scuba diving); (c) obesity; (d) food hygiene; (e) infectious diseases; (f) nutrition; (g) various toxic gases and materials.	x	
Intoxication: (a) prescribed medication; (b) tobacco; (c) alcohol and drugs; (d) caffeine; (e) self-medication.	x	
Basic aviation psychology		
Human information processing		
Attention and vigilance: (a) selectivity of attention; (b) divided attention.	x	
Perception: (a) perceptual illusions; (b) subjectivity of perception;	x	

(c) processes of perception.		
Memory: (a) sensory memory; (b) working or short term memory; (c) long term memory to include motor memory (skills).	x	
Human error and reliability		
Reliability of human behaviour	x	
Error generation: social environment (group, organisation)	x	
Decision making		
Decision-making concepts:	x	
(a) structure (phases); (b) limits; (c) risk assessment; (d) practical application.		
Avoiding and managing errors: cockpit management		
Safety awareness: (a) risk area awareness; (b) situational awareness.	x	
Communication: verbal and non-verbal communication	x	
Human behaviour		
Personality and attitudes: (a) development; (b) environmental influences.	x	
Identification of hazardous attitudes (error proneness)		
Human overload and underload		
Arousal	x	
Stress: (a) definition(s); (b) anxiety and stress; (c) effects of stress.	x	
Fatigue and stress management: (a) types, causes and symptoms of fatigue; (b) effects of fatigue; (c) coping strategies; (d) management techniques; (e) health and fitness programmes;	x	
3 METEOROLOGY		
The atmosphere		
Composition, extent and vertical division		
Structure of the atmosphere	x	
Troposphere	x	
Air temperature		
Definition and units	x	
Vertical distribution of temperature	x	
Transfer of heat	x	
Lapse rates, stability and instability	x	
Development of inversions and types of inversions	x	
Temperature near the Earth's surface, surface effects, diurnal and seasonal variation, effect of clouds and effect of wind	x	
Atmospheric pressure		
Barometric pressure and isobars	x	
Pressure variation with height	x	
Reduction of pressure to mean sea level	x	

Relationship between surface pressure centres and pressure centres aloft	x
Air density	
Relationship between pressure, temperature and density	x
ICAO Standard Atmosphere (ISA)	
ICAO standard atmosphere	x
Altimetry	
Terminology and definitions	x
Altimeter and altimeter settings	x
Calculations	x
Effect of accelerated airflow due to topography	x
Wind	
Definition and measurement of wind	
Definition and measurement	x
Primary cause of wind	
Primary cause of wind, pressure gradient, Coriolis force and gradient wind	x
Variation of wind in the friction layer	x
Effects of convergence and divergence	x
General global circulation	
General circulation around the globe	x
Local winds	
Anabatic and katabatic winds, mountain and valley winds, venturi effects, land and sea breezes	x
Mountain waves (standing waves, lee waves)	
Origin and characteristics	x
Turbulence	
Description and types of turbulence	x
Formation and location of turbulence	x
Thermodynamics	
Humidity	
Water vapour in the atmosphere	x
Mixing ratio	x
Temperature / dew point, relative humidity	x
Changes of state of aggregation	
Condensation, evaporation, sublimation, freezing and melting, latent heat	x
Adiabatic processes	
Adiabatic processes, stability of the atmosphere	x
Clouds and Fog	
Cloud formation and description	
Cooling by adiabatic expansion and by advection	x
Cloud types and cloud classification	x
Influence of inversions on cloud development	x
Fog, mist, haze	
General aspects	x
Radiation fog	x
Advection fog	x
Steaming fog	x
Frontal fog	x
Orographic fog (hill fog)	x
Precipitation	
Development of precipitation	
Processes of development of precipitation	x
Types of precipitation	
Types of precipitation, relationship with cloud types	x

Air masses and fronts	
Air masses	
Description, classification and source regions of air masses	x
Modifications of air masses	x
Fronts	
General aspects	x
Warm front, associated clouds and weather	x
Cold front, associated clouds and weather	x
Warm sector, associated clouds and weather	x
Weather behind the cold front	x
Occlusions, associated clouds and weather	x
Stationary front, associated clouds and weather	x
Movement of fronts and pressure systems, life cycle	x
Changes of meteorological elements at a frontal wave	x
Pressure systems	
Anticyclone	
Anticyclones, types, general properties, cold and warm anticyclones, ridges and wedges, subsidence	x
Non frontal depressions	
Thermal-, orographic-, polar depressions, troughs	x
Climatology	
Climatic zones	
General seasonal circulation in the troposphere	x
Typical weather situations in the mid-latitudes	
Westerly situation	x
High pressure area	x
Flat pressure pattern	x
Local winds and associated weather	
e.g. Foehn	x
Flight hazards	
Icing	
Conditions for ice accretion	x
Types of ice accretion	x
Hazards of ice accretion, avoidance	x
Turbulence	
Effects on flight, avoidance	x
Wind shear	
Definition of wind shear	x
Weather conditions for wind shear	x
Effects on flight, avoidance	x
Thunderstorms	
Conditions for and process of development, forecast, location, type specification	x
Structure of thunderstorms, life history, squall lines, electricity in the atmosphere, static charges	x
Electrical discharges	x
Development and effects of downbursts	x
Thunderstorm avoidance	x
Inversions	
Influence on aircraft performance	x
Hazards in mountainous areas	
Influence of terrain on clouds and precipitation, frontal passage	x
Vertical movements, mountain waves, wind shear, turbulence, ice accretion	x
Development and effect of valley inversions	x

	Visibility reducing phenomena	
	Reduction of visibility caused by precipitation and obscuration	x
	Reduction of visibility caused by other phenomena	x
	Meteorological information	
	Observation	
	Surface observations	x
	Radiosonde observations	x
	Satellite observations	x
	Weather radar observations	x
	Aircraft observations and reporting	x
	Weather charts	
	Significant weather charts	x
	Surface charts	x
	Information for flight planning	
	Aviation weather messages	x
	Meteorological broadcasts for aviation	x
	Use of meteorological documents	x
	Meteorological warnings	x
	Meteorological services	
	World area forecast system and meteorological offices	x
4	**COMMUNICATIONS**	
	VFR COMMUNICATIONS	
	Definitions	
	Meanings and significance of associated terms	x
	ATS abbreviations	x
	Q-code groups commonly used in RTF air-ground communications	x
	Categories of messages	x
	General operating procedures	
	Transmission of letters	x
	Transmission of numbers (including level information)	x
	Transmission of time	x
	Transmission technique	x
	Standard words and phrases (relevant RTF phraseology included)	x
	R/T call signs for aeronautical stations including use of abbreviated call signs	x
	R/T call signs for aircraft including use of abbreviated call signs	x
	Transfer of communication	x
	Test procedures including readability scale	x
	Read back and acknowledgement requirements	x
	Relevant weather information terms (VFR)	
	Aerodrome weather	x
	Weather broadcast	x
	Action required to be taken in case of communication failure	x
	Distress and urgency procedures	
	Distress (definition, frequencies, watch of distress frequencies, distress signal and distress message)	x
	Urgency (definition, frequencies, urgency signal and urgency message)	x
	General principles of VHF propagation and allocation of frequencies	x
5	**PRINCIPLES OF FLIGHT**	
5.1	**PRINCIPLES OF FLIGHT: AEROPLANE**	
	Subsonic aerodynamics	
	Basics concepts, laws and definitions	

Laws and definitions:		x
(a) conversion of units; (b) Newton´s laws; (c) Bernoulli's equation and venturi; (d) static pressure, dynamic pressure and total pressure; (e) density; (f) IAS and TAS.		
Basics about airflow:		x
(a) streamline; (b) two-dimensional airflow; (c) three-dimensional airflow.		
Aerodynamic forces on surfaces:		x
(a) resulting air force; (b) lift; (c) drag; (d) angle of attack.		
Shape of an aerofoil section		x
(a) thickness to chord ratio; (b) chord line; (c) camber line; (d) camber; (e) angle of attack.		
The wing shape:		x
(a) aspect ratio; (b) root chord; (c) tip chord; (d) tapered wings; (e) wing planform.		
The two-dimensional airflow about an aerofoil		
Streamline pattern		x
Stagnation point		x
Pressure distribution		x
Centre of pressure		x
Influence of angle of attack		x
Flow separation at high angles of attack		x
The lift – alpha graph		x
The coefficients		
The lift coefficient Cl: the lift formula		x
The drag coefficient Cd: the drag formula		
The three-dimensional airflow round a wing and a fuselage		
Streamline pattern:		x
(a) span-wise flow and causes; (b) tip vortices and angle of attack; (c) upwash and downwash due to tip vortices; (d) wake turbulence behind an aeroplane (causes, distribution and duration of the phenomenon).		
Induced drag:		x
(a) influence of tip vortices on the angle of attack; (b) the induced local alpha; (c) influence of induced angle of attack on the direction of the lift vector; (d) induced drag and angle of attack.		
Drag		
The parasite drag:		x
(a) pressure drag; (b) interference drag;		

(c) friction drag.	
The parasite drag and speed	x
The induced drag and speed	x
The total drag	x
The ground effect	
Effect on take off and landing characteristics of an aeroplane	x
The stall	
Flow separation at increasing angles of attack: (a) the boundary layer: (1) laminar layer; (2) turbulent layer; (3) transition. (b) separation point; (c) influence of angle of attack; (d) influence on: (1) pressure distribution; (2) location of centre of pressure; (3) C_L; (4) C_D; (5) pitch moments. (e) buffet; (f) use of controls.	x
The stall speed: (a) in the lift formula; (b) 1g stall speed; (c) influence of: (1) the centre of gravity; (2) power setting; (3) altitude (IAS) (4) wing loading; (5) load factor n: (i) definition; (ii) turns; (iii) forces. The initial stall in span-wise direction: (a) influence of planform; (b) geometric twist (wash out); (c) use of ailerons.	x
Stall warning: (a) importance of stall warning; (b) speed margin (c) buffet; (d) stall strip; (e) flapper switch; (f) recovery from stall.	x
Special phenomena of stall: (a) the power-on stall; (b) climbing and descending turns; (c) t-tailed aeroplane; (d) avoidance of spins: (1) spin development; (2) spin recognition; (3) spin recovery. (e) ice (in stagnation point and on surface): (1) absence of stall warning; (2) abnormal behaviour of the aircraft during stall.	x

C$_L$ augmentation		
Trailing edge flaps and the reasons for use in take-off and landing: (a) influence on C$_L$ - α-graph; (b) different types of flaps; (c) flap asymmetry; (d) influence on pitch movement.	x	
Leading edge devices and the reasons for use in take-off and landing		
The boundary layer		
Different types: (a) laminar (b) turbulent.	x	
Special circumstances		
Ice and other contamination: (a) ice in stagnation point; (b) ice on the surface (frost, snow and clear ice); (c) rain; (d) contamination of the leading edge; (e) effects on stall; (f) effects on loss of controllability; (g) effects on control surface moment; (h) influence on high lift devices during take-off, landing and low speeds.	x	
Stability Condition of equilibrium in steady horizontal flight		
Precondition for static stability	x	
Equilibrium: (a) lift and weight; (b) drag and thrust.	x	
Methods of achieving balance		
Wing and empennage (tail and canard)	x	
Control surfaces	x	
Ballast or weight trim	x	
Static and dynamic longitudinal stability		
Basics and definitions: (a) static stability, positive, neutral and negative; (b) precondition for dynamic stability; (c) dynamic stability, positive, neutral and negative.	x	
Location of centre of gravity: (a) aft limit and minimum stability margin; (b) forward position; (c) effects on static and dynamic stability.	x	
Dynamic lateral or directional stability		
Spiral dive and corrective actions	x	
Control General		
Basics, the three planes and three axis	x	
Angle of attack change	x	
Pitch control		
Elevator	x	
Downwash effects	x	
Location of centre of gravity	x	
Yaw control		
Pedal or rudder	x	
Roll control		
Ailerons: function in different phases of flight	x	
Adverse yaw	x	
Means to avoid adverse yaw:	x	

(a) frise ailerons;		
(b) differential ailerons deflection.		
Means to reduce control forces		
Aerodynamic balance:	x	
(a) balance tab and anti-balance tab;		
(b) servo tab.		
Mass balance		
Reasons to balance: means	x	
Trimming		
Reasons to trim	x	
Trim tabs	x	
Limitations Operating limitations		
Flutter	x	
V_{fe}	x	
V_{no}, V_{ne}	x	
Manoeuvring envelope		
Manoeuvring load diagram:	x	
(a) load factor;		
(b) accelerated stall speed;		
(c) V_a;		
(d) manoeuvring limit load factor or certification category.		
Contribution of mass	x	
Gust envelope		
Gust load diagram	x	
Factors contributing to gust loads	x	
Propellers		
Conversion of engine torque to thrust		
Meaning of pitch	x	
Blade twist	x	
Effects of ice on propeller	x	
Engine failure or engine stop		
Windmilling drag	x	
Moments due to propeller operation		
Torque reaction	x	
Asymmetric slipstream effect	x	
Asymmetric blade effect	x	
Flight mechanics		
Forces acting on an aeroplane		
Straight horizontal steady flight	x	
Straight steady climb	x	
Straight steady descent	x	
Straight steady glide	x	
Steady coordinated turn:	x	
(a) bank angle;		
(b) load factor;		
(c) turn radius;		
(d) rate one turn.		
6	**OPERATIONAL PROCEDURES**	
	General Operation of aircraft:	
	ICAO Annex 6, General requirements	
	Definitions	x
	Applicability	x
	Special operational procedures and hazards (general aspects)	x

	Noise abatement	
	Noise abatement procedures	x
	Influence of the flight procedure (departure, cruise and approach)	x
	Runway incursion awareness (meaning of surface markings and signals)	x
	Fire or smoke	
	Carburettor fire	x
	Engine fire	x
	Fire in the cabin and cockpit, (choice of extinguishing agents according to fire classification and use of the extinguishers)	x
	Smoke in the cockpit and (effects and action to be taken) and smoke in the cockpit and cabin (effects and actions taken)	
	Windshear and microburst	
	Effects and recognition during departure and approach	x
	Actions to avoid and actions taken during encounter	x
	Wake turbulence	
	Cause	x
	List of relevant parameters	x
	Actions taken when crossing traffic, during take-off and landing	x
	Emergency and precautionary landings	
	Definition	x
	Cause	x
	Passenger information	x
	Evacuation	x
	Action after landing	x
	Contaminated runways	
	Kinds of contamination	x
	Estimated surface friction and friction coefficient	
7	**FLIGHT PERFORMANCE AND PLANNING**	
7.1	**MASS AND BALANCE: AEROPLANES OR HELICOPTERS**	
	Purpose of mass and balance considerations	
	Mass limitations	
	Importance in regard to structural limitations	x
	Importance in regard to performance limitations	x
	CG limitations	
	Importance in regard to stability and controllability	x
	Importance in regard to performance	x
	Loading Terminology	
	Mass terms	x
	Load terms (including fuel terms)	x
	Mass limits	
	Structural limitations	x
	Performance limitations	x
	Baggage compartment limitations	x
	Mass calculations	
	Maximum masses for take-off and landing	x
	Use of standard masses for passengers, baggage and crew	x
	Fundamentals of CG calculations	
	Definition of centre of gravity	x
	Conditions of equilibrium (balance of forces and balance of moments)	x
	Basic calculations of CG	
	Mass and balance details of aircraft	
	Contents of mass and balance documentation	

		X
	Datum and moment arm	X
	CG position as distance from datum	X
	Extraction of basic mass and balance data from aircraft documentation	
	BEM	X
	CG position or moment at BEM	X
	Deviations from standard configuration	X
	Determination of CG position	
	Methods	
	Arithmetic method	X
	Graphic method	X
	Load and trim sheet	X
	General considerations	X
	Load sheet and CG envelope for light aeroplanes and for helicopters	X
7.2	**PERFORMANCE: AEROPLANES**	
	Introduction	
	Performance classes	X
	Stages of flight	X
	Effect of aeroplane mass, wind, altitude, runway slope and runway conditions	X
	Gradients	X
	SE aeroplanes	
	Definitions of terms and speeds	X
	Take-off and landing performance	
	Use of aeroplane flight manual data	X
	Climb and cruise performance	
	Use of aeroplane flight data	X
	Effect of density altitude and aeroplane mass	X
	Endurance and the effects of the different recommended power or thrust settings	X
	Still air range with various power or thrust settings	X
7.3	**FLIGHT PLANNING AND FLIGHT MONITORING**	
	Flight planning for VFR flights VFR navigation plan	
	Routes, airfields, heights and altitudes from VFR charts	X
	Courses and distances from VFR charts	X
	Aerodrome charts and aerodrome directory	X
	Communications and radio navigation planning data	
	Completion of navigation plan	X
	Fuel planning	
	General knowledge	X
	Pre-flight calculation of fuel required	
	Calculation of extra fuel	X
	Completion of the fuel section of the navigation plan (fuel log) and calculation of total fuel	X
	Pre-flight preparation AIP and NOTAM briefing	
	Ground facilities and services	X
	Departure, destination and alternate aerodromes	X
	Airway routings and airspace structure	X
	Meteorological briefing	
	Extraction and analysis of relevant data from meteorological documents	
	ICAO flight plan (ATS flight plan)	
	Individual flight plan	
	Format of flight plan	X
	Completion of the flight plan	X
	Submission of the flight plan	X
	Flight monitoring and in-flight re-planning	

	Flight monitoring	
	Monitoring of track and time	x
	In-flight fuel management	x
	In-flight re-planning in case of deviation from planned data	
8	**AIRCRAFT GENERAL KNOWLEDGE**	
8.1	**AIRFRAME AND SYSTEMS, ELECTRICS, POWERPLANT AND EMERGENCY EQUIPMENT**	
	System design, loads, stresses, maintenance	
	Loads and combination loadings applied to an aircraft's structure	x
	Airframe	
	Wings, tail surfaces and control surfaces	
	Design and constructions	x
	Structural components and materials	x
	Stresses	x
	Structural limitations	x
	Fuselage, doors, floor, wind-screen and windows	
	Design and constructions	x
	Structural components and materials	x
	Stresses	x
	Structural limitations	x
	Flight and control surfaces	
	Design and constructions	x
	Structural components and materials	x
	Stresses and aero elastic vibrations	x
	Structural limitations	
	Hydraulics	
	Hydromechanics: basic principles	x
	Hydraulic systems	x
	Hydraulic fluids: types and characteristics, limitations	x
	System components: design, operation, degraded modes of operation, indications and warnings	x
	Landing gear, wheels, tyres and brakes	
	Landing gear	
	Types and materials	
	Nose wheel steering: design and operation	x
	Brakes	
	Types and materials	x
	System components: design, operation, indications and warnings	x
	Wheels and tyres	
	Types and operational limitations	x
	Flight controls	
	Mechanical or powered	x
	Control systems and mechanical	x
	System components: design, operation, indications and warnings, degraded modes of operation and jamming	x
	Secondary flight controls	
	System components: design, operation, degraded modes of operation, indications and warnings	x
	Anti-icing systems	
	Types and operation (pitot and windshield)	x
	Fuel system	
	Piston engine	

	System components: design, operation, degraded modes of operation, indications and warnings	x
Electrics		
Electrics: general and definitions		
	Direct current: voltage, current, resistance, conductivity, Ohm's law, power and work	x
	Alternating current: voltage, current, amplitude, phase, frequency and resistance	x
	Circuits: series and parallel	x
	Magnetic field: effects in an electrical circuit	x
Batteries		
	Types, characteristics and limitations	x
	Battery chargers, characteristics and limitations	x
Static electricity: general		
	Basic principles	x
	Static dischargers	x
	Protection against interference	x
	Lightning effects	x
Generation: production, distribution and use		
	DC generation: types, design, operation, degraded modes of operation, indications and warnings	x
	AC generation: types, design, operation, degraded modes of operation, indications and warnings	x
Electric components		
	Basic elements: basic principles of switches, circuit-breakers and relays	x
Distribution		
	General: (a) bus bar, common earth and priority; (b) AC and DC comparison.	x
Piston engines		
General		
	Types of internal combustion engine: basic principles and definitions	x
	Engine: design, operation, components and materials	x
Fuel		
	Types, grades, characteristics and limitations	x
	Alternate fuel: characteristics and limitations	x
Carburettor or injection system		
	Carburettor: design, operation, degraded modes of operation, indications and warnings	x
	Injection: design, operation, degraded modes of operation, indications and warnings	x
	Icing	x
Air cooling systems		
	Design, operation, degraded modes of operation, indications and warnings	x
Lubrication systems		
	Lubricants: types, characteristics and limitations	x
	Design, operation, degraded modes of operation, indications and warnings	x
Ignition circuits		
	Design, operation, degraded modes of operation	x
Mixture		
	Definition, characteristic mixtures, control instruments, associated control levers and indications	x
Propellers		
	Definitions and general: (a) aerodynamic parameters;	x

	(b) types;	
	(c) operating modes.	
	Constant speed propeller: design, operation and system components	
	Propeller handling: associated control levers, degraded modes of operation, indications and warnings	x
	Performance and engine handling	
	Performance: influence of engine parameters, influence of atmospheric conditions, limitations and power augmentation systems	x
	Engine handling: power and mixture settings during various flight phases and operational limitations	x
8.2	**INSTRUMENTATION**	
	Instrument and indication systems	
	Pressure gauge	
	Different types, design, operation, characteristics and accuracy	x
	Temperature sensing	
	Different types, design, operation, characteristics and accuracy	x
	Fuel gauge	
	Different types, design, operation, characteristics and accuracy	x
	Flow meter	
	Different types, design, operation, characteristics and accuracy	x
	Position transmitter	
	Different types, design, operation, characteristics and accuracy	x
	Torque meter	
	Design, operation, characteristics and accuracy	x
	Tachometer	
	Design, operation, characteristics and accuracy	x
	Measurement of aerodynamic parameters	
	Pressure measurement	
	Static pressure, dynamic pressure, density and definitions	x
	Design, operation, errors and accuracy	x
	Temperature measurement: aeroplane	
	Design, operation, errors and accuracy	x
	Displays	
	Altimeter	
	Standard atmosphere	x
	The different barometric references (QNH, QFE and 1013.25)	x
	Height, indicated altitude, true altitude, pressure altitude and density altitude	x
	Design, operation, errors and accuracy	x
	Displays	x
	Vertical speed indicator	
	Design, operation, errors and accuracy	x
	Displays	x
	Air speed indicator	
	The different speeds	
	IAS, CAS, TAS: definition, usage and relationships	x
	Design, operation, errors and accuracy	x
	Displays	x
	Magnetism: direct reading compass	
	Earth magnetic field	x
	Direct reading compass	
	Design, operation, data processing, accuracy and deviation	x
	Turning and acceleration errors	x
	Gyroscopic instruments	

	Gyroscope: basic principles	
	Definitions and design	x
	Fundamental properties	x
	Drifts	x
	Turn and bank indicator	
	Design, operation and errors	x
	Attitude indicator	
	Design, operation, errors and accuracy	x
	Directional gyroscope	
	Design, operation, errors and accuracy	x
	Communication systems	
	Transmission modes: VHF, HF and SATCOM	
	Principles, bandwidth, operational limitations and use	x
	Voice communication	
	Definitions, general and applications	x
	Alerting systems and proximity systems	
	Flight warning systems	
	Design, operation, indications and alarms	x
	Stall warning	
	Design, operation, indications and alarms	x
	Integrated instruments: electronic displays	
	Display units	
	Design, different technologies and limitations	x
9	**NAVIGATION**	
9.1.	**GENERAL NAVIGATION**	
	Basics of navigation	
	The solar system	
	Seasonal and apparent movements of the sun	x
	The earth	
	Great circle, small circle and rhumb line	x
	Latitude and difference of latitude	x
	Longitude and difference of longitude	x
	Use of latitude and longitude co-ordinates to locate any specific position	x
	Time and time conversions	
	Apparent time	x
	UTC	x
	LMT	x
	Standard times	x
	Dateline	x
	Definition of sunrise, sunset and civil twilight	x
	Directions True north, magnetic north and compass north	x
	Compass deviation	x
	Magnetic poles, isogonals, relationship between true and magnetic	x
	Distance	
	Units of distance and height used in navigation: nautical miles, statute miles, kilometres, metres and ft	x
	Conversion from one unit to another	x
	Relationship between nautical miles and minutes of latitude and minutes of longitude	x
	Magnetism and compasses General principles	
	Terrestrial magnetism	
	Resolution of the earth's total magnetic force into vertical and horizontal	x

components		
Variation-annual change		x
Aircraft magnetism		
The resulting magnetic fields		x
Keeping magnetic materials clear of the compass		x
Charts General properties of miscellaneous types of projections		
Direct Mercator		x
Lambert conformal conic		x
The representation of meridians, parallels, great circles and rhumb lines		
Direct Mercator		x
Lambert conformal conic		x
The use of current aeronautical charts		
Plotting positions		x
Methods of indicating scale and relief (ICAO topographical chart)		x
Conventional signs		x
Measuring tracks and distances		x
Plotting bearings and distances		
DR navigation		
Basis of DR		
Track		x
Heading (compass, magnetic and true)		x
Wind velocity		x
Air speed (IAS, CAS and TAS)		x
Groundspeed		x
ETA		x
Drift and wind correction angle		x
DR position fix		x
Use of the navigational computer		
Speed		x
Time		x
Distance		x
Fuel consumption		x
Conversions		x
Air speed		x
Wind velocity		x
True altitude		x
The triangle of velocities		
Heading		x
Ground speed		x
Wind velocity		x
Track and drift angle		
Measurement of DR elements		
Calculation of altitude		x
Determination of appropriate speed		x
In-flight navigation		
Use of visual observations and application to in-flight navigation		x
Navigation in cruising flight, use of fixes to revise navigation data		
Ground speed revision		x
Off-track corrections		x
Calculation of wind speed and direction		x
ETA revisions		x
Flight log		x
9.2	**RADIO NAVIGATION**	

Basic radio propagation theory		
Antennas		
Characteristics		x
Wave propagation		
Propagation with the frequency bands		x
Radio aids		
Ground DF		
Principles		x
Presentation and interpretation		x
Coverage		x
Range		x
Errors and accuracy		x
Factors affecting range and accuracy		x
NDB / ADF		
Principles		x
Presentation and interpretation		x
Coverage		x
Range		x
Errors and accuracy		x
Factors affecting range and accuracy		x
VOR		
Principles		x
Presentation and interpretation		x
Coverage		x
Errors and accuracy		x
Factors affecting range and accuracy		x
DME		
Principles		x
Presentation and interpretation		x
Coverage		x
Range		x
Errors and accuracy		x
Factors affecting range and accuracy		x
Radar		
Ground radar		
Principles		x
Presentation and interpretation		x
Coverage		x
Range		x
Errors and accuracy		x
Factors affecting range and accuracy		x
Secondary surveillance radar and transponder		
Principles		x
Presentation and interpretation		x
Modes and codes		x
GNSS		
GPS, GLONASS OR GALILEO		
Principles		x
Operation		x
Errors and accuracy		x
Factors affecting accuracy		x

Sovereignty - The authority of a state to govern itself.

AIR LAW

How does ICAO recognise sovereignty?

Every state has complete and exclusive sovereignty over airspace above its territory

If a person on the ground is seriously injured by a component falling from an aircraft in flight what does ICAO consider this to be?

An aircraft accident

According to Annex 2, who is responsible for the safe conduct of a flight?

The PIC

Who is responsible for notifying an accident?

The pilot or operator

What did the Chicago Convention establish?

- Except for scheduled services, all aircraft of contracting states may fly into or across the territory of another contracting state without permission
- Entry and exit rules are based upon those of the state in question
- Compliance with flight rules is the responsibility of both the state of registry and the over flight state
- When an aircraft lands in another state the authorities there have the right to search the aircraft.
- On landing spare parts and oil remaining on board are exempt from customs duty

What is the territory of a state?

Land areas and adjacent territorial waters

Are International Standards mandatory?

Yes

What is a flying machine?

A power-driven heavier than air aircraft

ANO - Air Navigation Order

C of A - Certificates of Airworthiness

AIR LAW

What documents must be carried by aircraft engaged in international aviation?

Certificate of Registration
Certificate of Airworthiness
Crew licences
Journey log book
Radio station licence
Passenger list with places of embarkation / destination
Cargo manifest

Who is responsible for the issue of a Certificate of Airworthiness?

The State, which approves the aircraft or an authorised representative

With respect to U.K. aircraft where do the provisions of the ANO and Rules of the Air apply?

Worldwide

In the U.K. which aircraft require noise certificates?

All except for certain Short Take-off and Landing (STOL) types

What is night?

Between the end of evening civil twilight and the beginning of morning civil twilight

If the aircraft or its equipment is repaired or modified in any way other than an approved manner does this affect the C of A?

Yes, it then ceases to be valid

How long must the aircraft weight schedule be preserved?

6 months after the next weighing

If a restricted C of A has been issued what must be done before flying to another state?

Permission must be obtained from that state

AIR LAW

If a full C of A has been issued in accordance with agreed standards will another state recognise this?

Yes

When must the certificate of registration be carried?

At all times

Who determines the continuing airworthiness of an aircraft?

The State of Registry

What safety equipment must be carried on every flight?

A fire extinguisher, first aid kit and spare fuses

When a PPL hires an aircraft from a flying club, who is responsible for ensuring that the weather is suitable and the aircraft is fit and complies with all relevant maintenance procedures?

The PPL hirer

To fly on an international flight who issues the pilot's licence?

The state of registry of the aircraft

An aerodrome to which an aircraft may proceed when the flight cannot land at the original destination is known as?

An alternate

Where can the airworthiness limitations be found?

In the flight manual and on cockpit placards

Of what material should the aircraft identification plate be made?

Fireproof metal

What radio and navigation equipment must be carried by an aircraft below FL100 in class D airspace in VFR or SVFR?

VHF communications

SEP - Single Engine Piston

AIR LAW

The privileges of the U.K. PPL may be found where?

In Schedule 8 of the ANO and PART-FCL

Which documents relate to flight crew licensing?

ICAO Annex 1 Personnel Licensing
PART-FCL 1

What is the maximum period of validity of a PART-FCL licence?

Indefinite

To re-validate a single pilot SEP class rating what must be done?

i   Either pass a proficiency check within 3 months preceding the expiry date, or
ii   Within 12 months preceding the expiry date complete 12 h including 6 h P1 and 12 take-offs and landings and complete a 1 h training flight with an instructor

To fly in command the licence holder must have?

The valid appropriate class or type rating

For how long is a single pilot SEP class rating valid?

2 years

How is solo, command and dual instruction time counted?

In full and must be in the same category of aircraft as the licence or rating sought

What medical certificate is required for the PPL?

Class 1 or 2

How long is a PART-MED Class 2 medical certificate is valid for?

60 months until the age of 40

AME - Aeromedical Examiner(s)

AIR LAW

When may an EASA licence holder transfer his licence from one state to another?

When employment or normal residency is established in that other state

When must chronic illness be reported?

On the 21st consecutive day

If a licence holder needs an operation what is the procedure?

Immediately seek the advice of the authority or an AME

If a licence holder suffers a serious injury what is the status of the medical certificate?

It is suspended

What should an aircraft, which has right of way, do?

Maintain heading and speed

How long before departure should a flight plan be submitted?

At least 60 min

If a long delay is expected what should the pilot do with respect to the flight plan?

Cancel the original and submit a new one

How do you file a flight plan from an aerodrome with no air traffic services unit?

By telephone or radio to the appropriate unit

Mode C transponder — Report pressure altitude.

AIR LAW

What are the light signals to aircraft?

		On the ground	In the air
	Green flashes	clear taxi	return to circuit and wait to land
	Steady green	clear take off	clear land
	Steady red	Stop	give way and keep circling
	Red flashes	move clear of landing strip	do not land
	White flashes	return to start	land after receiving green

What is the parking area for an aircraft known as?

The aircraft stand

What is the loading area for an aircraft known as?

The apron

What frequency should an intercepted aircraft use to contact the intercept control unit?

121.5 MHz or 243 MHz

How is vertical position expressed above the transition level?

As flight level

How is vertical position expressed below the transition altitude?

As altitude

How is vertical position expressed in the transition layer?

Flight level when climbing and altitude when descending

When should a serviceable transponder be operated?

At all times during flight

When should Mode C on a transponder be operated?

At all times unless otherwise directed by ATC

AIP- Aeronautical Information Package

SNOWTAM- Snow Warning To Airmen

AIR LAW

In which class of airspace is advisory service given?

Class F

An AIP supplement should be printed on what colour paper?

Conspicuous, preferably yellow

For how long is a SNOWTAM valid?

No longer than 24 h

What does wet mean with respect to a runway?

The runway is soaked with no standing water

What does water patches mean with respect to a runway?

There are significant patches of standing water

What is the term used for a forced landing on water?

Ditching

What is radar vectoring?

Navigational guidance to the aircraft based on headings given by ground radar

In which section of the AIP would differences from ICAO Standards be found?

GEN

How are mandatory signs depicted?

White writing on a red background

Runway end lights should be?

Fixed unidirectional red lights showing in the direction of the runway

AIR LAW

What is the ICAO recommended colour for runway markings?

White

What is the ICAO recommended colour for taxiway markings?

Yellow

Runway threshold lights should be?

Fixed unidirectional green lights showing in the direction of the approach

How are information signs depicted?

Yellow writing on a black background or black writing on a yellow background

High intensity obstacle lights must be used on obstacles of what height?

Greater than 150 m

What is the colour of high intensity obstacle lights?

Flashing white

How are obstacles lit?

Below 150 m   -   lit by night if necessary by medium intensity flashing red
150 m or more   -   lit day and night by flashing white

When should search and rescue services be provided?

On a 24 h basis

Can an aircraft be re-fuelled with passengers on board?

Yes for AVTUR; provided it is attended by qualified personnel to initiate an evacuation if necessary and two-way communication is maintained. No; for AVGAS

AIR LAW

When should a passenger briefing be done?

Before take-off

Where must portable fire extinguishers be placed on an aircraft?

Pilot's compartment and each compartment separate from the pilot's compartment which is not readily accessible to flight crew

When are life jackets required?

Over water and more than 50 NM from shore; en-route and beyond gliding distance from shore

When are life rafts required?

If the flight is more than 100 NM from land

How is the vertical position of an aircraft described?

Altitude   QNH set (above mean sea level)
Height   QFE set (above airfield which issued the QFE)
Flight level   1013 set (Flight level)

What is the purpose of the regional QNH?

This is the lowest QNH in a particular altimeter setting region and will normally mean that the actual altitude is greater than that indicated

What is the function of Approach Control?

To provide a service for all arriving or departing flights

When encountering severe weather what should the pilot do?

Immediately inform ATC by a special air report (AIREP)

What is de-icing?

A procedure by which frost, ice and snow is removed from aircraft in order to provide clean surfaces

AIR LAW

What are the braking action coefficients?

Measured / calculated coefficient	Estimated surface friction
0.40 and above	GOOD – 5
0.39 to 0.36	GOOD/MEDIUM – 4
0.35 to 0.30	MEDIUM – 3
0.29 to 0.26	MEDIUM/POOR – 2
0.25 and below	POOR -1
9 - unreliable	UNRELIABLE – 9

When may aircraft fly in formation?

When the commanders of the aircraft have agreed to do so

What is the order of priority with respect to collision avoidance?

Aeroplanes / helicopters give way to airships / balloons / gliders
Airships give way to gliders and balloons
Gliders give way to balloons
Powered aircraft give way to aircraft towing

When two aircraft are converging which aircraft must give way?

The one, which has the other on its right (in the air and on the ground).
At night the one which sees the red navigation light

When approaching head on what is the correct avoiding action?

Each aircraft should alter course to the right (in the air and on the ground)

When overtaking what is the procedure?

The overtaking aircraft should alter course to the right in the air and to the left on the ground

AIR LAW

What constitutes overtaking?

When the faster aircraft is converging within 70° of the extended centreline of the overtaken aircraft.

What is the procedure when take-offs and landings are not confined to a runway?

On both take-off and landing leave other aircraft clear on the left

Which gives way a tractor towing an aircraft or an aircraft?

An aircraft

What is the function of Air Traffic Services?

To expedite flow, to prevent collisions, to provide advice and information and assist search and rescue

What does the following symbol indicate?

Take-off and land parallel with the shaft towards the crossbar

What do white crosses spaced less than 300 m apart on a manoeuvring area indicate?

The section between the crosses is unfit for aircraft use

AIR LAW

What is the quadrantal rule?

Above 3000' aircraft should be flown at levels shown in the diagram according to their magnetic track

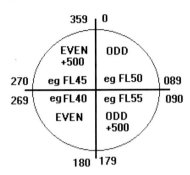

An aircraft is on a track of 269 T with variation 5 W, the Minimum Safety Altitude is 3100' and the QNH 999. What would be the lowest appropriate quadrantal level?

FL45

Explanation:
Magnetic track is 269 + 5 = 274 M
This is between 270 and 359 therefore the lowest FL is FL 45.
The QNH is 999 so for terrain clearance purposes at FL 45 the altitude will be 4500 - (14 x 27') = 4122' which is above 3100' and therefore safe

What   does   the   following symbol indicate?

Direction of take-off and landing may be different

AIR LAW

At night what lights must a free balloon display?

A steady red light in all directions

At night what lights must a glider display?

Either the same as a free balloon or a powered aircraft

Under what conditions may simulated instrument flight be practised?

- Dual controls fitted and functioning
- Safety pilot in the second seat
- If safety pilot's view is inadequate an observer must be carried

Can the IR(R) rating be used internationally?

Yes, only within the EU

What service is provided in Class D airspace?

- IFR from IFR and information regarding VFR
- VFR receive traffic information on all flights
- IFR and VFR are permitted and subject to ATC

What is the minimum weather for VFR flight in class D and E airspace below FL 100?

1500 m horizontally
1000' vertically from cloud
5 km minimum visibility

AIR LAW

What service is provided in Class F airspace?

- IFR flights receive advisory service
- IFR and VFR receive flight information if requested
- IFR and VFR are permitted

What service is provided in Class G airspace (the open FIR)?

Flight information service and alerting service

What is the VMC minima in Class G airspace below 3000' with the IAS equal to or less than 140 KT?

Clear of cloud
In sight of the surface
1500 m visibility minimum

What is the alerting service?

A search and rescue service available to all aircraft known to be operating in the FIR

What is the alert phase?

When apprehension exists as to the safety of an aircraft and its occupants

What is the distress phase?

This follows the alert phase when:
- Further attempts to establish contact fail
- Fuel is considered to be exhausted
- Information is received that the aircraft might be forced to land

AIR LAW

What is a control area (CTA)?

Controlled airspace extending upwards from a specified lower limit above the earth

Who is responsible for alerting individual SAR units?

The rescue co-ordination centre

What is a terminal control area (TMA)?

A control area in the vicinity of one or more major aerodromes

What is a control zone (CTZ)?

Controlled airspace extending from the surface to a specified vertical limit

What is the lateral limit of a control zone?

At least 5 NM from the centre of the aerodrome in the direction from which approaches may be made

What is TORA?

Take-Off Run Available, the length of runway declared available and suitable for the ground run of an aircraft taking-off

What is ASDA?

Accelerate Stop Distance Available, TORA plus stopway available

What is TODA?

Take-Off Distance Available, TORA plus clearway

AIR LAW

What is the conspicuity transponder code?

7000

What is the hijack / unlawful interference transponder code?

7500

What is the radio failure transponder code?

7600

What is the emergency transponder code?

7700

If given an unsuitable clearance by ATC what should the pilot do?

Request a revised clearance for example a different heading or level in order to maintain VMC

If a pilot considers the fuel state to be critical what radio call should be made to alert ATC of the need for priority?

A MAYDAY or PAN PAN call depending on the circumstances

Which document covers EASA licensing requirements?

PART-FCL 1

What are the recency requirements for a PPL to carry passengers?

Conduct 3 take-offs and landings within the previous 90 days

Can a PPL holder be paid for flying?

No

AIR LAW

What are some of the provisions of U.K. ANO Rule 5?

The minimum height must be 1500' above the highest fixed object within 600 m (2000') or to alight clear of the congested area whichever is the higher.

An aircraft shall not fly closer than 500' to any person, vessel, vehicle or structure

What are some of the conditions of Special VFR flight?

The pilot may be absolved from the 1500' rule but not the alight clear rule.

ATC provides separation from other SVFR traffic but terrain clearance is the pilot's responsibility

AIRCRAFT GENERAL KNOWLEDGE

What is a stringer?

A part of the aircraft fuselage structure used to give the fuselage its shape and, in some types of structure, to provide a small portion of the fuselage strength

What is a former?

A former defines the basic shape and strengthens the fuselage

What is a rib?

A rib defines the wing profile and transmits the aerodynamic load on the skin to the spars

What is a monocoque fuselage?

A monocoque fuselage has no internal structure, the entire load being taken by the skin

What are tyre creep marks?

Painted indicators on the wheel flange and the tyre sidewall to enable the amount of tyre rotation relative to the wheel to be measured

What are control locks for?

To ensure that no damage is caused to the flight controls on the ground in strong or gusty wind conditions

What are control stops for?

To limit control deflection in flight thus avoiding over stressing the aircraft

When should MOGAS not be used?

$\geq 20\ ^0 C$
$\geq 6000'\ PA$

The vacuum gauge reads zero, however the suction instruments read normally what does this mean?

The vacuum gauge is broken

AIRCRAFT GENERAL KNOWLEDGE

What would happen if the vacuum pump filter became blocked?

The vacuum relief valve allows air into the pump and the instruments do not receive operating air

What is conventional current flow?

+ve   supply to series
-ve   return to supply

What does "load" usually refer too?

Power (Watts) or current (Amperes)

What is the formula for total amperage in a circuit?

Total amperage   =   sum of all the amperages

If a resistance is removed from a series circuit what happens to total current?

Current drawn increases

What is a TRIP free circuit breaker?

Free to trip thus can be held in and will trip

What is a non TRIP free circuit breaker?

Not free to trip
If held in circuit does not trip and damage could result

What is battery density checked with?

A hydrometer

What does connecting batteries in parallel do to capacity and voltage?

Increases capacity but has no effect on voltage

AIRCRAFT GENERAL KNOWLEDGE

What does connecting batteries in series do to capacity and voltage?

Increases voltage but has no effect on capacity

Where is the generator voltage regulated?

In the field coil

If the generator is battery supplied, what happens if you switch the battery master OFF?

The generator will be de-excited and will cease to produce power

If the aircraft electrical system is 24 volts, what will be the generator regulation?

28 volts

How is generator failure indicated?

Decrease or discharge on ammeter and generator warning red light ON

When does the generator warning light illuminate?

When the generator voltage falls below the battery voltage and the cut-out has opened

How is a battery prevented from discharging back through a generator?

With a reverse current cut-out switch

When might the reverse current circuit breaker trip?

When the reverse current cut out fails to operate

When closed what colour do thermal trip circuit breakers show?

Black

AIRCRAFT GENERAL KNOWLEDGE

In electrical circuits how do short circuits occur?

Single pole   -   conductor to aircraft structure
Double pole   -   bridging of conductors

What is an Earth return circuit?

The negative return from electrical components is sent via the aircraft structure

During refuelling what must be bonded?

The aircraft must be bonded to Earth
The fuel nozzle must be bonded to the fuel tank

What type of current are batteries charged by?

DC

If two 12 volt batteries are connected in parallel what will the voltage be?

12 volts

What will two 12 volt 60 ampere h batteries connected in parallel produce?

12 volts 120 ampere hours

What will two 12 volt 40 ampere h batteries connected in parallel produce?

12 volts 80 ampere hours

What will three 12 volt 40 ampere h batteries connected in series produce?

36 volts 40 ampere h

What will a 40 ampere hour battery deliver?

At the 10 h rate it will deliver 4 amps per h for 10 h

AIRCRAFT GENERAL KNOWLEDGE

What will a 60 ampere hour battery deliver?

At the 10 h rate it will deliver 6 amps per h for 10 h

When a battery is nearly fully discharged what happens to voltage and current?

Voltage under load and current drawn reduce

What does the ammeter show if the generator is operating normally?

Needle shows a positive reading

What does the ammeter show if the generator fails?

Needle shows a negative or zero reading depending on the gauge

Should you fly with a flat battery?

No, it is not recommended because the battery may not charge correctly in flight

If manifold air density decreases what happens to engine power?

Engine power decreases

How is power indicated on piston and turbine engines?

Piston   -   rpm and manifold pressure
Turbine   -   rpm and torque meter

What is the effect of throttle opening and closing on MAP and air density in the manifold?

Opening the throttle   -   increases MAP and air density
Closing the throttle   -   decreases MAP and air density

In a normally aspirated engine what is the MAP when the engine is running?

Below atmospheric due to the pressure drop across the throttle plate

AIRCRAFT GENERAL KNOWLEDGE

In a normally aspirated engine as the throttle is closed what happens to MAP?

The pressure drop increases and MAP falls

In a normally aspirated engine what is the MAP when the engine is stopped?

Atmospheric

What is power developed at the engine shaft known as?

Brake (shaft) horse power

The power output of a piston engine at sea level

Increases as the RPM increases

What is a square engine?

One where stroke = bore
Stroke being the distance a piston moves between TDC and BDC
Bore being the diameter of the cylinder

What is compression ratio?

Compression ratio = Total volume BDC to total volume at TDC

How many times do the valves open during the normal Otto cycle?

Once

What is the four stroke Otto cycle?

Induction (ICPE)
Compression
Power
Exhaust

What are the numbers of power strokes in the Otto cycle?

One power stroke per cycle of four strokes

AIRCRAFT GENERAL KNOWLEDGE

How many times does the crankshaft revolve in the Otto cycle?

Twice

How are valves opened mechanically?

Cams on the camshaft rotate and push on tappets at the end of push rods which rotate the rocker to depress the poppet valves

How many times does the camshaft revolve in the Otto cycle?

Once (i.e. at half the crankshaft rate)

What is the firing order for a 4 stroke engine?

1342 or
1243

What is the stoichiometric air : fuel ratio?

15:1

What are different types of fuel?

	Colour	DERD
AVGAS 100L	Green	2485
AVGAS 100LL	Blue	2475

What colour smoke and flames are related to mixture settings?

Rich	Black smoke	Red flame	
Normal		Blue flame	
Weak		Yellow flame	Detonation

What is the slow running jet?

A hole next to the throttle plate to increase fuel flow

What happens when the throttle is opened rapidly?

The airflow responds more rapidly than the fuel flow causing a weak cut

AIRCRAFT GENERAL KNOWLEDGE

How is a weak cut cured?

With an accelerator pump

Where does priming fuel go?

To the inlet manifold

What causes pre-ignition?

Hot spots causing an early burning of the fuel / air mixture.

What causes detonation?

Too weak a mixture or too hot or high pressure air / fuel charge

How may high cylinder head temperatures be reduced?

By enriching the mixture

Where is the filter in the dry sump system?

Between the engine and the scavenge pump

Where are oil pressure and temperature measured?

In the oil supply line after the pump before the engine

Where is the oil cooler?

Between the scavenger pump and the oil reservoir. It has a by-pass, which is automatically activated at a pre-set pressure

You have a problem in flight with the oil system?

Land as soon as possible to investigate the problem

What causes blue / grey smoke?

Oil burning due to scraper rings failing

AIRCRAFT GENERAL KNOWLEDGE

What is the electrical source for the ignition system in a piston engine aircraft?

The magneto

What is a magneto?

A rotating permanent magnet surrounding a 1^0 low tension coil which forms an AC Generator and a transformer with a contact breaker to trigger a high voltage

Magneto switched off

The primary circuit is closed and earthed

If the connection between the switch and the magneto fails.

The engine will continue to run when both magneto switches are off

On starting how is the spark adjusted?

On one magneto it is retarded also the spark may be too weak so it is intensified

What is used to retard and intensify the spark?

An impulse starter - coiled spring
or a low tension booster and retard breaker

What are manifold or boost pressure gauges calibrated in?

Manifold - inches of Hg
Boost - psi

What is rated altitude?

Full throttle height at rated power

What turns a magneto off?

Turning the ignition to OFF closes the primary circuit and causes it to earth

AIRCRAFT GENERAL KNOWLEDGE

What are the conditions most favourable for the formation of serious carburettor icing?

As high as +25 °C, greater than 35% relative humidity, descent power set

Where is information about MOGAS written?

CAA airworthiness certificates

What could happen if a fuel strainer is left open?

Fuel starvation could occur

What is the function of the idle cut-off valve?

It cuts off the fuel and stops the engine at any RPM

Why does the propeller angle vary from hub to tip?

The blade angle reduces from hub to tip make the blade angle of attack efficient throughout its whole length

What is geometric pitch?

The theoretical distance a propeller should move forward in one revolution (i.e. slip is zero)

What are the forces acting on a propeller?

Thrust, torque and centrifugal

What is pitch (blade) angle?

The angle between the blade chord line and the plane of rotation

If a propeller rotates clockwise when viewed from inside the aircraft which way will the aircraft yaw on take-off?

To the left

AIRCRAFT GENERAL KNOWLEDGE

If IAS is increased what happens to RPM with a fixed pitch propeller?

RPM increases

At what speed are fixed pitch propellers designed for maximum efficiency?

Cruise speed

What happens to rpm during the take off run with a fixed pitch propeller?

It increases due to increasing efficiency of the blade angle of attack

What happens to rpm with a fixed pitch propeller if the nose is raised in flight?

It decreases

What is a variable pitch propeller?

A propeller whose pitch changes to maintain a constant angle of attack at all speeds

After engine failure, if feathering was not available what action should be taken?

Select fully coarse

What are the errors of an altimeter?

Error	Reason	Correction
Barometric	sea-level pressure not being 1013.25 hPa	use sub-scale
Lag	friction and inertia	None
Instrument	manufacture and use	Card
Temperature	ISA temp structure deviation	none (CRP-5)
Pressure	Position or static error	error made +ve for safety by tilting static vent into wind

AIRCRAFT GENERAL KNOWLEDGE

What is the effect of blocked static inlet on an altimeter?

Static blocked gives constant reading

What is the construction of an altimeter?

Static fed to sealed case containing partially evacuated capsule(s) held distended with spring
A bimetallic strip corrects for temperature changes in the instrument itself not for ISA temp difference, which is known as temperature error

What is transition altitude?

The altitude at or below which the aircraft is controlled with respect to height above mean sea level

What is transition level?

The lowest flight level available for use above the transition altitude

What is the transition layer?

The airspace between transition altitude and transition level

What do you set on your altimeter when transiting the transition layer?

Climbing   -   1013.25 hPa
Descending -   QNH

What is the resulting difference in pressure in an unpressurised aircraft where the alternate static source uses cabin air?

The alternate static pressure will be lower than that outside the aircraft.

What is the construction of an ASI?

Pitot pressure is fed to a closed capsule and static pressure is fed to the case. A rocking shaft and a rocking sector transfers the capsule movement to an indicator

On an ASI when is indicated air speed equal to true air speed?

At ISA MSL density (1225 g / m^3)

AIRCRAFT GENERAL KNOWLEDGE

What happens with pressure blockages of the ASI?

	In a descent	In a climb
Pitot blocked	under reads	over reads
Static blocked	over reads	under reads
Both blocked	nil happens	

What is the colour coding of the ASI?

White		Flap operating range (Vso-Vfe)
Green		Normal operating range (Vs1-Vno)
Amber		Caution range (Vno-Vne)
Red radial line	—	Vne

What are the errors of an ASI?

Error	Reason	Correction
Density	ISA not 1225 g / m^3	Pressure altitude and cOAT using CRP-5
Compressibility	RAM effect at >300 KT	CRP-5
Pressure	Position or static error	tabulated for set height, weight and speed only
Instrument	manufacture and use	

What is pressure error dependent on?

All up weight, height and IAS

What happens to density error of an ASI in the climb?

It increases

What are the relationships between the different airspeeds?

IAS corrected for instrument and pressure error is RAS
RAS corrected for compressibility error is EAS
EAS corrected for density error is TAS

AIRCRAFT GENERAL KNOWLEDGE

What is take-off safety speed?

A speed giving at least 20% margin over the stall speed

What does a VSI measure?

Rate of change of static pressure with height

What is the construction of a VSI?

Static fed to an open metering unit and a sealed capsule all within a sealed case

What are the errors of a VSI?

Lag
Instrument
Pressure (Position or static)

If the static is blocked what will a VSI read?

Zero

What is apparent wander?

Earth rotation occurring at 15° / h

How do you correct for gross drift in a DGI?

Use the caging knob then realign in level unaccelerated flight

What type of gyro does an artificial horizon have?

Vertical axis Earth tied displacement gyro

What is the construction and principle of an artificial horizon?

The vertical axis Earth tied gyro maintains an horizon bar horizontal at all times and is carried in a rotor housing or shroud which forms the inner gimbal.
In the climb a guide pin drives the horizon bar down
In the descent a guide pin drives the horizon bar up
Roll motion of the aircraft rotates the instrument case

AIRCRAFT GENERAL KNOWLEDGE

How does an air driven artificial horizon remain erect?

The base of the gyro is pendulously weighted correcting for gross topple
Air jets, exhaust ports and pendulous vanes maintain the vertical
correcting for fine topple

How does an electrical artificial horizon remain erect?

With mercury switches and torque motors
Fast erect button can be used in any attitude in unaccelerated flight

What are the errors of an artificial horizon?

It is pendulously-mounted so has turning and acceleration errors
Mercury tilt switches are subject to acceleration errors
Linear errors:
Acceleration -   false climb and starboard roll
Deceleration -   false descent and port roll
Angular errors:
Maximum error after 180° of turn
Minimum on completion of 360° of turn

How are the errors of artificial horizons limited?

Slow acting torque motors
Fast acceleration pitch and roll gravity cut-out switches
Faster rpm gyros leading to more rigidity

What is the construction of a turn and balance indicator?

It has two parts:
The turn indicator - A horizontal axis rate gyro with gyro axis
athwartships
Balance indicator - ball in a tube

How does the turn indicator work in the turn?

Movement in roll is possible only and is restrained by springs which
produce secondary precession in the direction of the original primary
force producing a steady indication on the pointer

How does the turn indicator work in the roll?

The gyro reacts to roll to keep the pointer at zero

AIRCRAFT GENERAL KNOWLEDGE

What is the rotor speed in a turn indicator?

10000 rpm

If the gyro rpm of the turn indicator is less than normal?

The aircraft rate of turn will be greater than that indicated

What are rate 1, 2 and 3 turns?

Rate 1	1 hemisphere (180°) per min	3° per sec
Rate 2	2 hemispheres per min	
Rate 3	3 hemispheres per min	

What forces is the ball in the balance indicator sensitive to?

Gravity and centrifugal force

What are the two styles of presentation of turn and balance indicators?

Needle and ball
Needle and needle

What is the relationship between bank angle, skid, slip and needle (ball) indications?

Ball Opposite direction of turn	Skid	Under-banked
Ball Same side as direction of turn	Slip	Over-banked

What are the turn formulae?

Turn angle $= 3°$ x rate of turn x time (s)

If the TBI gyro is running slowly how will this affect the turn?

It will under-read therefore you will go past your turn

What is the bank angle for a rate 1 turn?

Bank angle $= \sqrt{TAS} + 7$

AIRCRAFT GENERAL KNOWLEDGE

How do you calculate the diameter of a rate 1 turn?

Diameter (NM)　　　　=　　　TAS (KT) / 100

How is radius of turn related to TAS and rate of turn?

Radius of turn is directly proportional to TAS
Radius of turn is inversely proportional to rate of turn

What gyro is in the turn co-ordinator?

Horizontal rate gyro mounted $30°$ off the horizontal

What is the difference in measurement of a TBI and a TC?

TBI has primary precession from turn but not bank
TC has primary precession from turn and bank but only offers rate

What are Z and H?

Z = vertical force producing dip (zero at equator, max at pole)
H = directive force (zero at pole, max at equator)

What is an isogonal?

A line of equal magnetic variation (accurate worldwide to $\pm2°$)

What is the line of zero magnetic variation called?

The agonic line

What are acceleration errors due to?

Vertical component of the Earth's field (Z)
Due to dip the centre of gravity is displaced nearer to the equator

How does the needle react to change of velocity on East / West headings?

Accelerating - indicates turn to nearer pole
Decelerating - indicates turn to equator

AIRCRAFT GENERAL KNOWLEDGE

Where are acceleration and turning errors at a maximum?

At the poles

How are compass turning errors minimised?

Turning errors are greatest when turning onto N and S. Use 'UNOS' (undershoot the turn onto N and overshoot the turn onto S)

After correction what is acceptable error in a compass?

Direct-reading compass - 3°

What is the effect of metal or magnetic material placed near the compass?

May cause large errors in the compass reading

What is the function of the liquid in the compass?

Supports the bar magnet, decreases friction and dampens oscillations

What is the standard ISA temperature lapse rate?

-1.98 °C per 1000' but for practical calculations use 2 °C per 1000'

The temperature at 5000' is +1° C what is this relative to ISA?

ISA -4 °C

What is the temperature and pressure at sea level in ISA?

+15 °C and 1013.25 hPa

If the temperature remains constant and the pressure increases how is the density affected?

It increases

If the moisture content of the air is increased how is the density affected?

It is reduced

AIRCRAFT GENERAL KNOWLEDGE

Does the C of A for an aircraft have an expiry date?

No

If a control system has received minor rectification away from base who is permitted to do the second inspection?

A pilot qualified on the type

What is the status of a CAA flight manual supplement?

It must be observed even if in conflict with the manufacturer's manual

How should maintenance performed by a PPL be recorded?

It must be entered in the aircraft logbook and signed by the PPL

What type of fires are water-based fire extinguishers suitable for?

Paper and fabric fires but not electrical fires

What is the safest extinguishant for a wheel fire?

Dry powder

If no specific instructions are given in the flight manual what are the immediate actions in the case of engine fire?

Throttle - close, fuel - off, cabin heat - close

What are the characteristics of carbon monoxide (CO)?

Colourless, odourless and poisonous

Following which type of aircraft could give rise to strong wake turbulence?

A heavy aircraft flying slowly

FLIGHT PERFORMANCE & PLANNING

Where are weight and C of G limitations stated?

C of A
Flight manual

What are the effects of the C of G being at Forward and Aft limits?

	C of G at forward limit	C of G at aft limit
Range	Decreased	Increased
Pitch	Stable in pitch	Unstable in pitch
Elevator pitch	Elevator pitch nose up reduced	Elevator pitch nose down reduced
Trim	Extra nose up trim needed giving more trim drag	Lower trim drag
Stalling speed	Increased stalling speed	Decreased stalling speed
Helicopters	Less forward speed and range of control	More strain on main shaft and less control

What is disposable load?

Passengers
Freight
Usable fuel and oil

How much does 1 Imp gallon of water weigh in lbs?

1 ImpG = 10 lbs

How much does 1 litre of water weigh in kg?

1 kg

How do you convert USG to ImpG?

$$1 \text{ USG} = \frac{5}{6} \text{ ImpG}$$

What are the fuel conversions?

kg	(x 2.2)	=	lbs
Imp gallons	(x 1.205)	=	US gallons
US gallons	(x 3.784)	=	litres
litres	(x S.G.)	=	kg

FLIGHT PERFORMANCE & PLANNING

How many quarts are there in a gallon?

4

What is the UTILITY category?

A small envelope located within the limits of the main envelope, in which the aircraft is loaded for semi-aerobatic manoeuvres

What is the NORMAL category?

Normal flying, no spinning, no aerobatics, bank angle < 60°

At what aircraft mass must passengers and baggage be weighed separately?

5700 kg or less

What is the formula for CG position from datum?

CG POSITION FROM DATUM = TOTAL MOMENT / TOTAL MASS

Take-off mass 2350 lb CG 87.2 in aft. Fuel burn 225 lb from tanks 79.0 in aft. What will be the landing mass and CG?

2125 lb CG 88.06 in aft

Explanation:				
Original take-off moment	2350 x 87.2	=	204920	(a)
Reduction due to fuel burn	225 x 79.0	=	17775	(b)
Landing moment (a) – (b)	204920 - 17775	=	187145	(c)
Landing mass	2350 – 225	=	2125	(d)
Landing CG (c) / (d)	187145 / 2125	=	88.06 in	

FLIGHT PERFORMANCE & PLANNING

How much does 300 litres of fuel with a SG 0.72 weigh in lbs?

475 lb

> Explanation:
>
> 1 litre of water weighs 1 kg therefore 300 litres fuel at 0.72 weighs
> 300 x 0.72 = 216 kg
> Convert kg to lbs
> 216 x 2.2 = 475 lb

What are some of the effects of overloading an aircraft?

Possible structural damage, poor handling, longer take-off and landing runs and reduced acceleration

What are gross mass / weight and zero fuel mass / weight?

Gross mass is the total mass of the aircraft at a particular time
Zero fuel mass is the total minus the fuel in the tanks

What does density altitude correspond to?

Ambient density, which depends on ambient air pressure and temperature

With increasing altitude, does a decrease in pressure or a decrease in temperature have the greater effect on density?

A decrease in pressure

What is the effect of wind on rate of climb, gradient and ground distance travelled, at constant IAS compared with still air conditions?

	rate of climb	gradient of climb	gradient of descent	ground distance travelled
headwind	no effect	increases	increases	decreases
tailwind	no effect	decreases	decreases	increases

FLIGHT PERFORMANCE & PLANNING

What is the slope of a 3000' runway having threshold elevations of 275' and 325'?

1.66%

Explanation:

The difference in height between the thresholds is 325 - 275 = 50'
The length is 3000' therefore the percentage gradient is:

(50 / 3000) x 100% = 1.66%

What determines gradient of climb, and at what calibrated airspeed is maximum gradient of climb achieved?

Excess thrust, since gradient of climb $= \dfrac{\text{Thrust - Drag}}{\text{Weight}} \times 100$

Vx

What determines rate of climb, and at what calibrated airspeed is maximum rate of climb achieved?

Excess power

Vy

What is absolute ceiling?

The altitude at which the theoretical rate of climb of an aeroplane is zero

FLIGHT PERFORMANCE & PLANNING

What speed is represented by the lowest point of the power required curve (A) for a piston propeller aeroplane?

Maximum endurance speed

What speed is represented by the intersection of the power required curve and the tangent to the curve drawn from the origin (B)?

Maximum range speed

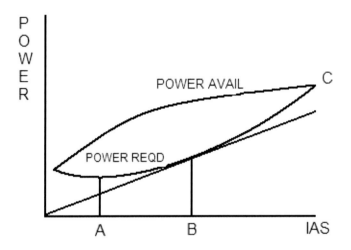

What is the effect of increasing the aircraft mass on stall speed, take-off run required, Vr, maximum range glide speed and landing distance required?

All increase

What is the effect of reduced air density on take-off distance?

It increases

What is the effect of an up-sloping runway?

It increases the take-off distance and reduces the landing distance

What is the effect of flap on rate of climb and stalling speed?

Reduces both

FLIGHT PERFORMANCE & PLANNING

What is the load factor?

The ratio of lift / weight (e.g. in a 60° bank turn the load factor is 2)

In a piston engine aircraft which is higher maximum range or maximum endurance speed?

Maximum range speed

Why should an aircraft land into wind?

To reduce the ground speed and therefore the landing distance required

An aircraft has a lift / drag ratio (C_L / C_D) of 5:1 how far can it glide from 2400'?

2 NM

Explanation:

To lose 2400' the distance travelled is 5 x 2400' = 12000'
Divide by 6080 to convert to NM 12000 / 6080 = 1.97 NM

What are the take-off and landing factors?

Use the public transport factor of 1.33 and refer to Table 1 TAKE-OFF and Table 2 LANDING:

TABLE 1 TAKE-OFF		
CONDITION	INCREASE IN TODR TO 50'	FACTOR
10% TAKE-OFF MASS	20%	1.2
+1000' ALTITUDE	10%	1.1
+10 °C INCREASE	10%	1.1
DRY GRASS	20%	1.2
WET GRASS	30%	1.3
2% UPHILL	10%	1.1
TAILWIND = 10% Vr	20%	1.2
SOFT SFC OR SNOW	25% or more	1.25 or more

FLIGHT PERFORMANCE & PLANNING

TABLE 2 LANDING		
CONDITION	INCREASE IN LDR from 50'	FACTOR
10% TAKE-OFF MASS	10%	1.1
+1000' ALTITUDE	5%	1.05
+10 °C INCREASE	5%	1.05
DRY GRASS	20% or more	1.2 or more
WET GRASS	30%-60% (short)	1.3 -1.6
2% DOWNHILL	10%	1.1
TAILWIND = 10% Vapp	20%	1.2
SNOW	25% or more	1.25 or more

030 FPP

What is the effect of a headwind during take-off?

The aircraft will reach take-off speed at a lower ground speed thus requiring a shorter ground roll

An aircraft has a landing configuration stall speed of 54 KT what is the minimum approach speed?

70 KT

> Explanation:
>
> Minimum approach speed is 1.3 x Vs
>
> 1.3 x 54 = 70 KT

What is the effect of using take-off flap?

Decreases the ground run and reduces the rate of climb

What is the effect of using full landing flap?

Lowers the approach speed and steepens the approach path

FLIGHT PERFORMANCE & PLANNING

What is the effect of using a higher than recommended approach speed?

It will increase the landing distance required by a considerable amount

What aids engine cooling in the climb?

High speed and a rich mixture

What is TORA?

The length of runway declared available and suitable for the ground run of an aircraft taking-off

What is ASDA?

TORA plus stopway available

What is TODA?

TORA plus clearway

Published performance figures are based upon what type of runway unless stated otherwise?

A hard, dry, level surface

What does an increase in pressure altitude do to take-off and landing distance?

Both are increased

What effect has a strong tailwind on the speed for best range compared with still air?

It reduces it

FLIGHT PERFORMANCE & PLANNING

TABLE 3 CLIMB TIME FUEL AND DISTANCE AT 2750 POUNDS

PRESS ALT feet	TEMP °C	IAS KT	RATE OF CLIMB fpm	FROM SEA LEVEL		
				TIME min	FUEL GAL	DIST NM
SL	15	83	950	0	0.0	0
1000	13	82	900	1	0.3	1
2000	11	81	850	3	1.0	4
3000	9	80	800	4	1.3	5
4000	7	79	750	5	1.7	7
5000	5	78	700	6	2.0	8
6000	3	77	650	8	2.7	10
7000	1	76	600	9	3.0	11
8000	-1	75	550	10	3.3	13
9000	-3	74	500	12	4.0	15
10000	-5	73	450	14	4.7	17
11000	-7	72	400	16	5.3	19
12000	-9	71	350	18	6.0	21

NOTE: ADD 1.5 GAL FOR START, TAXI & TAKE-OFF

Refer to Table 3: What is the time, fuel and distance to climb from 2000' to 7000' at 2750 lb?

6 min, 2.0 gal and 7 NM

Explanation:

The method is to subtract the figures in the 2000' row from the figures in the 7000' row.

9-3 = 6 min, 3-1 = 2 gal, 11-4 = 7 NM

Refer to Table 3 what is the time, fuel and distance to climb from sea level SL to 5000' at 2750 lb?

6 min, 3.5 gal and 8 NM

Explanation:

Read directly the figures from the 5000' row but remember to add 1.5 gal in accordance with the note at the foot of the table

FLIGHT PERFORMANCE & PLANNING

TABLE 4 CRUISE PERFORMANCE

PRESS ALT	RPM	20°C BELOW STANDARD TEMP			STANDARD TEMP			20°C ABOVE STANDARD TEMP		
		BHP	KTAS	GPH	BHP	KTAS	GPH	BHP	KTAS	GPH
1000	2300	*******	*******	*******						
	2200	80	115	10.5	77	113	8.2	73	111	7.9
	2100	75	111	9.6	73	112	7.9	70	109	7.7
	2000	70	107	8.7	69	111	7.6	67	107	7.5
	1900	65	103	7.8	65	110	7.3	64	105	7.3
3000	2300	*******	*******	*******						
	2200	77	117	8.2	73	115	7.9	71	113	8
	2100	73	115	7.9	70	114	7.7	69	112	7.9
	2000	69	113	7.6	67	113	7.5	67	111	7.8
	1900	65	111	7.3	64	112	7.3	65	110	7.7
5000	2300	*******	*******	*******						
	2200	77	119	8.2	76	117	8	72	115	7.9
	2100	73	118	7.9	74	116	7.9	71	114	7.7
	2000	69	117	7.6	72	115	7.8	70	113	7.5
	1900	65	116	7.3	70	114	7.7	69	112	7.3

NOTE: TABLE 6 IS FOR AIRCRAFT WITH SPEED FAIRINGS
WITHOUT SPEED FAIRINGS REDUCE KIAS BY 2 KT

Refer to Table 4 for an aircraft at 3000' on a standard day cruising at 2100 rpm calculate the BHP, KTAS and GPH for an aircraft with and without speed fairings.

With fairings 70 BHP, 114 KT and 7.7 GPH
Without fairings 70 BHP, 112 KT and 7.7 GPH

Explanation:

From the intersection of the 3000' / 2100 rpm row and the standard temperature column read the values directly for the aircraft with speed fairings. For the aircraft without speed fairings deduct 2 KT from the KIAS

FLIGHT PERFORMANCE & PLANNING

TABLE 4 MAX RATE OF CLIMB AT 2750 POUNDS

ALTITUDE	CLIMB IAS	-10°C	0 °C	+10	+20 °C
SL	81	900	850	740	700
2000	78	875	825	690	650
4000	76	775	740	600	550
6000	75	480	450	430	400
8000	74	400	390	400	380
10000	72	320	300	290	280
12000	72	200	***	***	***

Refer to Table 4 for an aircraft mass of 2750 lb: What is the maximum rate of climb for an aircraft at 4000' with a temperature of +5 °C?

670 fpm

Explanation:
In the 4000' row interpolate between 0°C (740 fpm) and +10°C (600 fpm) to obtain 670 fpm

HUMAN PERFORMANCE

How does the percentage of oxygen vary with altitude?

Remains constant but the reduced pressure makes breathing difficult

Which gas mainly controls human respiration?

The level of carbon dioxide in the blood

With respect to respiration the healthy body is more sensitive to changes in oxygen or carbon dioxide?

Carbon dioxide

What do carbon monoxide and oxygen combine with in the blood?

Haemoglobin

What is the function of the circulatory system?

To move blood around the body

For how long after blood donation should a pilot refrain from flying?

24 h

What is hypoxia?

Lack of oxygen

What are the first effects of hypoxia?

Loss of inhibitions and difficulty with mental tasks

What are characteristic symptoms of hypoxia?

Reduced consciousness, impaired judgement, muscular impairment, sensory loss memory impairment and personality change

What is the Time of Useful Consciousness?

The time available for a pilot to perform useful tasks without a supplementary oxygen supply and before hypoxia sets in

HUMAN PERFORMANCE

What are the symptoms of hyperventilation?

Dizziness, tingling fingers and lips, anxiety and visual disturbance

What causes hyperventilation?

Over-breathing due to anxiety, motion sickness, vibration and heat

A person showing symptoms of hypoxia at low altitude may be suffering from what?

Hyperventilation

How can hyperventilation be treated?

By re-breathing carbon dioxide via a paper bag
Calming the affected person down to restore the normal breathing rate

Which part of the eye is sensitive to light?

The retina

Effective lookout is best achieved by?

Short regular eye movements across the field of view

Whilst operating in an empty sky a pilot's eyes will focus where?

1 to 2 m ahead

What should a pilot ensure when adjusting the seat position?

Before flight that the seat is locked in the optimum position and avoid the danger of restricting the field of view on the approach by having the seat too low

How should aircraft seating be adjusted for the design eye position indication?

Prior to flight for a position suitable for all phases of flight

How long does night adaptation take?

30 - 40 min

PUBLISHED BY CATS LTD.

040 HPL

HUMAN PERFORMANCE

How is maximum visual acuity achieved at night?

By looking slightly to the side of the object by about $10°$

→ A light aircraft is closing head on with a fast military jet how does the image of the fast jet change with time?

Very little change initially making it very difficult to detect but a rapid growth when the aircraft become very close

→ A light aircraft (100 KT) is closing head on with a fast military jet (460 KT) with an in-flight visibility of 6 km what duration of time is there to take avoiding action?

21 s

Explanation:
Convert 6 km to NM on the navigation computer = 3.2 NM
Add the two speeds to obtain closing speed 100 + 460 = 560 KT
Calculate time (3.2 / 560) x 60 x 60 = 21 s

With regard to visual illusions what does a narrower than expected runway cause?

You think that you are high on approach and you descend early resulting in an undershoot hazard

With regard to visual illusions what does a wider than expected runway cause?

You think that you are low on approach and you descend late resulting in an overshoot hazard

With regard to visual illusions what does low visibility cause?

Runway appears dim or far away and you tend to overshoot

With regard to visual illusions what might a pilot perceive during a level acceleration?

A belief that the nose is pitching up

HUMAN PERFORMANCE

With regard to visual illusions what might a pilot perceive during a level deceleration?

A belief that the nose is pitching down

With regard to visual illusions what does rain on a windscreen cause?

Rain magnifies lights and they appear closer which tends to cause an undershoot

With regard to visual illusions what is the effect if an object is smaller than expected?

It seems to be more distant

With regard to visual illusions what is the effect if the approach and runway lights are very bright?

An early descent resulting in being too low

Regarding illusions what may a sloping cloud base cause a pilot to do?

Bank the aircraft

→**What should you do if you experience an illusion of movement during flight?**

Trust the aircraft instruments

What is the auditory hearing range?

20 – 20000 Hz

What is the function of the Eustachian tube?

To allow the middle ear pressure to equalise with ambient air pressure

What is vertigo?

The illusion of movement

HUMAN PERFORMANCE

Which of the following are measures to prevent and / or overcome spatial disorientation and / or vertigo in flight?

Always refer to flight instruments rather than somatosensory information

What causes air-sickness and what are its symptoms?

A mismatch between visual and vestibular sensory inputs

→**The stroboscopic effect of propeller or rotor blades adversely affects some people what is the best course of action?**

Sunglasses should be worn and the eyes closed if possible

What is the main danger associated with the use of non-prescription drugs?

Performance may be dangerously degraded and any pilot using such drugs should seek advice from an AME

Why should a pilot not fly with a cold?

Barotrauma may result from a blocked Eustachian tube not allowing the pressure between the middle ear and atmosphere to equalize potentially resulting in a burst ear drum

Should a pilot suffering from a cold or influenza fly in any type of aircraft even if pressurized?

No

What is the major contaminating source in foodstuffs?

Contaminated drinking water

→**What actions should be taken to avoid contamination?**

Boil or chlorinate water or use bottled water
Food prepared with contaminated water, ice, dairy products and unwashed vegetables should be avoided

What is the major cause of in-flight incapacitation?

Gastro-enteritis

PUBLISHED BY CATS LTD.   78   © 2015

HUMAN PERFORMANCE

Is a pilot suffering from gastro-enteritis fit to fly?

No

What is the major epidemic disease spread by mosquitoes that kills the most people globally?

Malaria

What are the harmful effects of using tobacco?

Risk factor in lung cancer and heart disease increase and may exacerbate hypoxia, degrade night vision and reduce g tolerance also susceptible to the effects of insufficient oxygen at a lower altitude

How long does it take for the body to eliminate one unit of alcohol?

1 h

What is one unit of alcohol?

One glass of wine, half pint of beer or one measure of spirit

What is the legal limit for Blood Alcohol Concentration?

20 mg / ml

For how many hours after consuming alcohol should a pilot not fly?

8 h, proportionally longer if large amounts have been consumed

Where may carbon monoxide be produced?

In cigarette smoke and from a leaking cockpit heater

What is a characteristic symptom of CO poisoning?

Cherry red lips

HUMAN PERFORMANCE

After being subjected to CO (exhaust gas) poisoning when would a pilot be fit to fly again?

After several days

To avoid decompression sickness for how long do you avoid flying for when you have been diving?

12 h when using compressed air to a depth of less than 30'
24 h when using compressed air to a depth of more than 30'

What is decompression sickness?

Nitrogen comes out of solution to form bubbles in body tissue when pressure is reduced

With regard to learning what are the behaviour patterns?

Skill-based	Learnt by practice Become motor programs Do not require conscious monitoring but it is recommended to monitor
Rule-based	Following procedures, for example checklists
Knowledge-based	Based on previous experience to address a novel problem

What are the divisions of the nervous system?

Central, Peripheral, and Autonomic

What is a disadvantage of the three pointer altimeter?

It can easily be misinterpreted

A good design of aircraft controls would incorporate what feature?

They should look and feel different

HUMAN PERFORMANCE

What percentage of aircraft accidents is thought to be due to human factors?

About 75%

What is stress a function of?

Perceived demand and perceived ability

What are the main dimensions of personality?

Stable and unstable
Extrovert and introvert

What are the main personalities reflected by?

Unstable introvert - sober and pessimistic
Unstable extrovert - aggressive and changeable
Stable introvert - controlled and thoughtful
Stable extrovert - responsive and easy-going

What are the most dangerous personality attitudes influencing pilot performance?

Anti-authority
Impulsive
Invulnerable
Macho
Resigned

A recently qualified pilot is flying with a much more experienced pilot whose course of action is considered unwise. What should the less experienced pilot do?

They should make their doubts known

What is being situationally aware?

When perception matches reality

What are the three levels of situational awareness?

Monitor, evaluate and anticipate i.e. consider all data, update its effect on the situation and plan ahead

HUMAN PERFORMANCE

How may a pilot maintain situational awareness?

By obtaining and considering all possible data whilst updating the situation and planning ahead

METEOROLOGY

What is the composition of the atmosphere?

N_2	78%
O_2	21%
Other	1%

What are the pressure levels with altitude?

30000'	300
18000'	500
10000'	700
Surface	1013 hPa

Where does most weather occur?

In the troposphere

What is Buys Ballot's law?

With your back to the wind, low pressure is to the left in the Northern hemisphere

As you fly towards low pressure what happens to true altitude if you fly a constant heading and QNH?

True altitude decreases (High to Low - Beware Below)

Flying in the northern hemisphere towards a region of lower pressure what drift would you experience?

Starboard (i.e. the aircraft drifts to the right)

Is moist air more or less dense than dry air?

Less dense

When are the warmest and coldest times of the day?

Warmest 1400 h
Coldest just after dawn

METEOROLOGY

What is relative humidity?

Percentage water saturation of air compared to what it could hold
Is a function of temperature unlike absolute humidity

Define a gale?

Minimum wind speed of 34 KT or more or gust of 43 KT or more

Where is Coriolis (geostrophic) force greatest and how does it deflect the wind?

Increases with latitude up to the N Pole and deflected right
Zero at the equator
Increases with latitude up to the S Pole and deflected left

What is the direction of the geostrophic wind?

Parallel to the isobars

What is the Pressure Gradient Force?

The force, which moves a parcel of air from high to low pressure

Where is the PGF (pressure gradient force) greatest?

At the equator (this leads to high wind speed which the Coriolis force deflects to cause tropical revolving storms) and decreases with latitude

What reduces the diurnal temperature range?

Strong wind to mix
Low cloud to blanket
Moist air to absorb long wave radiation

What are the backing factors at the SFC compared to the 2000' geostrophic wind?

	Day		Night	
Land	-20° backed	1/2 speed	-40° backed	1/3 speed
Sea	-15° backed 2/3 speed			

METEOROLOGY

What are the levels for clouds in temperate regions?

High   16500' – 40000'
Med   6500' - 23000'
Low   SFC - 6500'

In stable air what type of cloud forms?

Stratus

In unstable air what type of cloud forms?

Cumulus or Stratocumulus

What type of clouds would be formed by orographic uplift?

In an unstable air mass clouds with considerable vertical development

Under what conditions does carburettor icing form?

-10°C to +30°C (most severe -2°C to +15°C), low engine power +60% humidity, high speed

What are the times for Thunderstorm development?

Development   20-30 min
Mature stage   40-60 min
Dissipating   2 h

What is the temperature band for lightning?

+10°C to -10°C

What are the avoidance distances for thunderstorms?

Flight level	Avoidance distance
250-300	15 NM
0-250	10 NM

What are the properties of air masses?

Same dew point, temperature and stability

METEOROLOGY

What is the ratio of ice accretion?

For every degree below freezing 1 / 80 rime and 79 / 80 clear
eg -3°C leads to 3 / 80 rime

What is rain ice?

Cold aircraft flies into rain

What is a METAR?

A surface actual report of weather conditions at an aerodrome and valid
for 2 h

What is a TAF?

A forecast of weather conditions at an aerodrome over a specified
period of time (9 h, 18 h, or 24 h)

What is VOLMET?

A verbal (often automated) report of actual weather conditions at
specific aerodromes which may be listened to on the VHF receiver of
your aircraft

How much notification must be given for a Special Forecast?

<500 NM - 2 h
≥500 NM - more than 2 h

What is fog?

Visibility less than 1000 m

What is mist?

Visibility 1000 m or more with reporting starting at 5000 m

What is haze?

Reduced visibility (if less than 1000 m cause must be given) (<5000 m)

METEOROLOGY

How is RVR reported?

Commences when visibility is less than 1500 m

What are the wind speeds for dew, fog, stratus and clearance?

<2 KT dew	2-8 KT fog	>8-10 KT stratus	15-20 KT clearance

What are the properties of highs?

Warm or cold refers to mean atmospheric temperature
Warm highs   fairly stationary
Cold highs   move at 20-25 KT

What are the characteristics of the Tropical maritime air mass?

Generally, warm, moist and stable.
Summer: ST and fog. Fair weather CU inland. Mod. - poor vis.
Winter: 8 oktas ST. DZ and advection fog. Mod. - poor vis

What are the characteristics of the Tropical continental air mass?

Hot, dry and stable. Summer only. Nil cloud. Nil ppt. Mod - poor vis. In haze. Sea fog possible if air tracks over North sea.

What are the slopes of cold and warm fronts?

Cold   1:50
Warm   1:150

How wide is the warm front rain belt and what cloud is present?

150 NM ahead. NS 8 oktas ST becoming BKN ST (fractostratus) near SFC position

050 MET

METEOROLOGY

What are the temp and pressure changes associated with fronts?

	Temp & dew point	Pressure	Wind	Cloud	Precipitation
Ahead of warm front	rises	Falls	Backs	CI, CS, AS also CU and ST	INT SLT RA approx 200-250 NM ahead
At warm front	rises	Falls	Veers	NS, BKN ST	MOD to HVY CONT RA close to front
In warm Sector	steady	Steady	Steady	ST and/or SC	INT SLT RA or DZ with hill fog
At cold front	falls	Falls	Veers	CU, CB BKN ST or NS poss. AC and CC	MOD to HVY RASH
Behind cold Front	falls	Rises	may back	CU, CB	RASH

What weather is associated with a trough?

Intense line squalls.
Either side of trough NSW with SCT CU
Sharp uplift of air in centre of trough causes CBs

What is the weather like in an anticyclone in the winter?

Radiation fog or poor visibility due to dust trapped under an inversion

How is windshear duration reported?

OCNL	<1/3 of the time
Intermittent	1/3 to 2/3 of the time
Continuous	>2/3 of the time

When is a windshear alert given?

Mean SFC wind at least 20 KT
SFC and gradient wind vector difference of 40 KT
CBs or heavy showers within 5 NM
Temp diff of 10°C between SFC and 1000

What is the average environmental lapse rate?

1.98°C per 1000' or 0.65°C per 100 m

METEOROLOGY

What is the International Standard Atmosphere?

Sea level +15°C, 1013.25 hPa, lapse rate -1.98°C / 1000' until 36,090'
then -56.5°C

What does CAVOK mean?

10 km or more visibility
No cloud below 5000' or minimum sector altitude whichever is the
greater
No significant weather in the vicinity of the airfield

Temperature at 4000' is +9°C how does this compare with ISA?

ISA + 2

Surface temperature and dewpoint are 25/10 at what height would the base of CU cloud be found?

6000' (temperature - dewpoint) / 2.5 gives the height in 1000s of ft

What does this symbol indicate?

Severe icing

What does this symbol indicate?

Thunderstorms

Backing when referred to a change in wind direction means what?

An anti-clockwise change in direction e.g. from 270° to 240°

Veering when referred to a change in wind direction means what?

A clockwise change in direction e.g. from 270° to 300°

When compared to the daytime wind the evening wind does what?

Backs and decreases

METEOROLOGY

Which winds are given in degrees magnetic?

Tower reported winds and ATIS

Which winds are given in degrees true?

METARs and TAFs

You are warned of possible windshear when approaching an airfield what should you do?

Delay the landing or divert to a more suitable airfield

An aircraft takes off from aerodrome A with the correct QNH 1010 set and lands at B (elevation 300' QNH 1002) without changing the altimeter subscale. What will the altimeter read?

516'

Explanation:
(The altimeter is 'over set' by 8 hPa and therefore over-reads by 8 x 27' = 216') 300' + 216' = 516'

What is the speed of the warm front relative to the cold front?

2/3

What is virga?

Precipitation which does not reach the ground giving the appearance of rods or fall-streaks below the base of clouds

NAVIGATION

What is a rhumb line?

A line of constant direction and cuts all meridians and parallels at the same angle

What is nearer the pole, a rhumb line or a great circle?

A great circle

A great circle constantly changes direction, at what point does it have the same direction as a rhumb line?

At the mid-meridian of the track

How many NM is 1° of latitude?

60 NM (1 min is 1 NM)

What are the fuel conversions?

kg	(x 2.2)	=	lbs
Imp gallons	(x 1.205)	=	US gallons
US gallons	(x 3.784)	=	litres
litres	(x S.G.)	=	kg

What are the distance conversions?

1 inch	=	2.54 cm	
1 NM	=	6080 feet	= 1852 m
1 SM	=	5280 feet	
1 km	=	3280 feet	

What is the formula for scale?

$$\text{Scale} = \frac{1}{D} = \frac{\text{Chart Length}}{\text{Earth Distance}}$$

How is latitude described?

Degrees, minutes and seconds North or South of the equator
e.g. 51°23' 45" N

NAVIGATION

How is longitude described?

Degrees, minutes and seconds East or West of the prime (Greenwich) meridian
e.g. 002°23' 45" W

What is the relationship between compass, magnetic and true heading?

Remember:

"Cadbury's Dairy Milk is Very Tasty" (C D M V T)
Starting from the right with true (T) direction add (if west) or subtract (if east) variation to give the magnetic (M) direction and add (if west) or subtract (if east) the deviation to give compass direction (C)

When is variation or deviation added?

When it is westerly.
There is the saying "Variation west magnetic best"; best in this case means the greatest.
For example the measured true track is 271 T and the variation is 5 W
271 + 5 = 276 so the magnetic track is 276 M

On a CRP flight computer how is the wind vector drawn?

Rotate until the wind direction is under the INDEX mark at the top put the TAS under the centre circle and draw down the wind speed with a pencil

What is drift?

The angle from heading to track
For example if the aircraft heading is 070 M and the track is 075 M the drift is 5° starboard (right)

What is true airspeed (TAS)?

The speed of the aircraft through the air

What is a knot?

1 NM per hour
For example 75 KT means 75 nautical miles per hour

NAVIGATION

What is groundspeed (GS)?

The speed of the aircraft over the ground

What is the effect of a headwind on groundspeed?

Groundspeed (GS) is reduced
For example if the TAS is 110 and the aircraft is flying into a 20 KT headwind the GS will be 90 KT

What is heading (HDG)?

The direction in which the nose of the aircraft points

What is track (TRK)?

The actual path that the aircraft flies over the ground

What is the relationship between speed time and distance?

GS = DISTANCE / TIME
where GS = Groundspeed

TIME = DISTANCE / GS

> For example if an aircraft has a groundspeed of 90 KT what is the time taken to cover 135 NM
>
> TIME = 135 / 90 = 1.5 h or 1 h 30 min

Where should track be measured on the 'half million' chart?

Midway between the departure and destination

NAVIGATION

How do you calculate cross wind components?

Method 1
Mathematically by multiplying the wind speed by the sine of the angle between the wind and the runway.

> Example:
>
> Surface wind is 240 / 20 on runway 27 (Runway 270 M)
>
> Cross wind = 20 x sin 30 = 20 x 0.5 = 10 KT

Method 2
- Use the lower square scale on the CRP navigation computer
- Put the centre circle on the top line of the lower squared section
- Rotate until surface wind direction is aligned with the INDEX
- Mark the wind cross below the centre circle
- Rotate until the runway direction is aligned
- Read the crosswind on the horizontal scale markings

If the maximum demonstrated cross wind component is 15 KT by how many degrees can a 25 KT wind differ from the runway direction to remain within limits?

37°

> Explanation:
>
> Use the lower square scale on the CRP navigation computer
> - Put the centre circle on the top line of the lower squared section
> - Rotate until surface 0 is aligned with the index
> - Mark the wind cross 25 KT below the centre circle
> - Rotate until the wind cross is on 15 on the horizontal scale
> - Read 37° on the heading index at the top

On the 1 : 500,000 ICAO aeronautical chart how are Maximum Elevation Figures shown?

As a two figure group in 100's feet over-printed in blue (with the second figure smaller than the first). For example **22** means two thousand two hundred feet

NAVIGATION

What is the U.K. quadrantal rule?

Outside controlled airspace a pilot should fly at specified levels according to the aircraft's magnetic track:

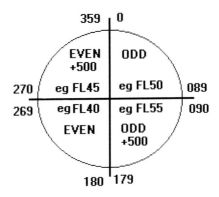

For example if the aircraft track is 345 M a suitable level might be FL 45 subject to terrain clearance requirements

For a VFR flight what terrain clearance should be allowed?

500' above all obstacles within 5 NM either side of track

What is LARS?

Lower Airspace Radar Service

What is a VRP?

A Visual Reference Point

What is the 1 in 60 rule?

A one degree track error will result in a 1 NM displacement from track after 60 NM

NAVIGATION

An aircraft is 2 NM off track after 30 NM what is the track error?

4°

Explanation:
If the aircraft continued with no correction then after 60 NM it would be 4 NM off track therefore by the 1 in 60 rule the track error is 4°

What are the glide clear rules (U.K. ANO Rule 5)?

A pilot must fly at or above 1500' above the highest fixed object within 600 m (2000') or at an altitude to enable the aircraft to glide clear in the event of engine failure whichever is the higher

How do you calculate fuel required for a flight rounded up to the nearest gallon?

Example:
1.5 US gallons for start, taxi run-up and take-off
Time to destination 1 h 15 min (8 US gallons / h)
Diversion time 30 min (8 US gallons / h)
1.5 US gallons for approach
45 min reserve

23 US Gallons

Explanation:	
Time to destination = 1 h 15 min at 8 USG / h requires	**10 USG**
Start, taxi, power checks and take-off	**1.5 USG**
Diversion = 30 min at 8 USG / = 4 USG	**4 USG**
Approach	**1.5 USG**
45 reserve at 8 USG / h	**6 USG**
Total	**23 USG**

NAVIGATION

How do you calculate the required rate of descent?

Example:
15 NM before aerodrome A an aircraft is at 4500' with a groundspeed of 90 KT. What rate of descent is required to be level at 2000' 5 miles before A?

375 fpm

Explanation:
Time available for the descent 10 NM (distance) at 90 KT = 6.66 min Altitude loss required is 4500 - 2000 = 2500' Rate of descent required is 2500 / 6.66 = 375 fpm

Refer to Table 2: How is payload calculated?

Table 2	
Aircraft basic empty weight	**1450 lb**
Pilot	**170 lb**
Fuel 50 USG (SG = 0.72)	**? lb**
Max weight authorised	**2450 lb**

What is the maximum payload which may be carried?

530 lb

Explanation:

Calculate the weight of the fuel:
    50 USG = 50 x 5/6 = 41.6 Imp Gal
    41.6 Imp Gal weighs 41.6 x 10 x 0.72 = 300 lb
Calculate (d) - (a) - (b) - (c)
2450 - 1450 -170 - 300 = 530 lb

What are the latest distance and time requirements for requesting MATZ penetration?

15 NM / 5 min

NAVIGATION

How are obstacle altitude and height depicted on the 1 : 500000 ICAO chart?

The upper figure in italics is the altitude above Mean Sea Level the figure in brackets is the height above the local ground level

How are customs airfields depicted on the 1 : 500000 ICAO chart?

With a pecked line around the name of the aerodrome and elevation

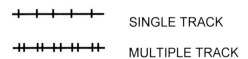

What does PPR mean?

Prior Permission Required

What does AIAA mean?

Area of Intense Aerial Activity

What colour is an aerodrome identification beacon?

Green with a two letter Morse code ident

How are railway tracks depicted?

┼─┼─┼─┼─┼─   SINGLE TRACK

╫─╫─╫─╫─╫─   MULTIPLE TRACK

060 NAV

NAVIGATION

How is an advisory route depicted?

A blue dashed line with a blue letter F in a blue square beside it

What does the following mean on the ICAO 1 : 500000 chart?

> D013/15
> OCNL/19

Danger area from the surface to 15000' AMSL active at times notified in the AIP and by NOTAM and with notification to 19000'

To what ceiling are glider sites referenced to on the ICAO 1 : 5000000 chart?

Altitude above mean sea level

When can VORs be used?

Day and Night

Which frequency band do VORs operate in?

VHF

What are the Q codes for bearings?

QDM	magnetic to	QUJ	true to
QDR	magnetic from	QTE	true from

What are the VDF bearing classifications?

A - $\pm 2°$
B - $\pm 5°$
C - $\pm 10°$

What degrades VDF accuracy?

Site and propagation errors

What is a QGH procedure?

A controller-interpreted letdown used by military giving headings
ATC gives HDGs to steer

NAVIGATION

What is a VDF let down?

QDMs given by ATC and pilot works out headings to steer

What distances and heights are air to ground communications limited to in the UK?

Tower	25 NM	4000'
Approach	25 NM	10000'

060 NAV

OPERATIONAL PROCEDURES

What is a microburst?

A sharp downdraught of cold air often associated with thunderstorms or virga

How may a microburst be detected?

ATS warning
SIGMET
Warnings from other pilots
An increase in IAS
An uninitiated climb

What can cause windshear?

Thunderstorms, frontal passage, virga, roll cloud, inversions

What happens to an aircraft during an approach with an increasing head wind?

Rate of descent decreases and airspeed increases

What happens to an aircraft during an approach with a decreasing head wind?

Rate of descent increases and airspeed decreases

What happens to an aircraft during climb out with an increasing tailwind?

Rate of descent decreases and airspeed decreases

What do holding points ensure?

Safe clearance between the aircraft holding and any aircraft passing in front of the holding aircraft

When can a taxiway hold line be crossed?

When clear left and right
When red stop bars are unlit
With ATC specific clearance

OPERATIONAL PROCEDURES

Who ultimately should determine the best runway for landing?

The pilot

When is a runway defined as being contaminated?

It has water patches

How should operations on contaminated runways be regarded?

Operations from contaminated runways, by all classes of aeroplane, should be avoided whenever possible

What does wet mean with respect to a runway?

The runway is soaked with no standing water

What does water patches mean with respect to a runway?

There are significant patches of standing water

What does flooded mean with respect to a runway?

Extensive standing water

What are the consequences of landing on a contaminated runway?

The coefficient of friction will be decreased, braking effectiveness will be reduced and landing distance will be increased

• When is wake turbulence created?

As soon as an aircraft produces lift or when a helicopter hovers

How far should you remain clear of hovering helicopters to avoid wake turbulence?

3 rotor diameters

What is wake turbulence?

The effect of the rotating air masses generated behind the wing tips of aircraft

OPERATIONAL PROCEDURES

Following which type of aircraft could give rise to strong wake turbulence?

A heavy aircraft at high angle of attack (or in the landing configuration), flying slowly in light wind conditions

What are the risk factors for wake turbulence?

Close parallel runways
Departing after another aircraft prior to the point at which it rotated
Crossing behind and below another aircraft in light wind conditions
Landing after the point at which another aircraft rotated

When is the word "HEAVY" used?

By aircraft in the heavy wake turbulence category immediately after the call sign in the initial call

What actions should be taken if there is smoke in the cockpit? 38

Inform ATC
Master switch OFF
Electrics OFF
Cabin heat OFF
Open window
Land at nearest aerodrome

What actions should be taken if there is smoke / flames from the 39 **engine during starting?**

Continue Cranking
Mixture LEAN
Fuel OFF
Throttle OPEN
If fire does not go out
Master switch OFF
Evacuate Aircraft

What are the evacuation procedures?

Inform ATC
Turn off all systems
Meet upwind of the aircraft

070 OPS

Distress call - Mayday x3

Emergency code - 7700

OPERATIONAL PROCEDURES

What is the term used for a forced landing on water? 33

Ditching

What method should be used for ditching?

Make a distress call
Squawk 7700
Head towards land or shipping
Attempt re-start
Plan to land parallel to swell

When should life jackets be inflated?

Once outside the aircraft before entering the water

What transponder code should be used for ditching?

7700

What is TORA?

Take-Off Run Available, the length of runway declared available and suitable for the ground run of an aircraft taking-off

What is ASDA?

Accelerate Stop Distance Available, TORA plus stopway available

What is TODA?

Take-Off Distance Available, TORA plus clearway

What is a clearway?

A defined rectangular area on the ground selected or prepared as a suitable area over which an aircraft may make a portion of its initial climb to a specified height

070 OPS

OPERATIONAL PROCEDURES

What is the definition of pilot in command?

The pilot designated by the operator or owner (general aviation) as being in command and charged with the safe conduct of flight

What is the definition of flight time?

The total time from the moment that an aeroplane moves for the purpose of taking off until the moment it finally comes to rest at the end of the flight

What should a pilot do if uncertain of position on a movement area?

Stop the aircraft unless on a runway and contact the ATS unit for assistance

What is night?

Between the end of evening civil twilight and the beginning of morning civil twilight

What are the light signals to aircraft?

		On the ground	In the air
	Green flashes	clear taxi	return to circuit and wait to land
	Steady green	clear take off	clear land
	Steady red	Stop	give way and keep circling
	Red flashes	move clear of landing strip	do not land
	White flashes	return to start	land after receiving green

What is an OPS manual?

A manual acceptable to the State of the Operator, containing normal, non-normal and emergency procedures, checklists, limitations, performance information, details of aircraft systems and other material relevant to the operation

070 OPS

OPERATIONAL PROCEDURES

What is General Aviation operation?

An aircraft operation other than commercial air transport or aerial work

Where may a pilot find details of noise abatement procedures?

In the AIP

PRINCIPLES OF FLIGHT

In level flight where do lift and weight act?

Lift acts through the Centre of Pressure
Weight acts through the Centre of Gravity

What is the angle of attack?

The angle between the chord line and the relative airflow

At zero angle of attack what forces will a cambered wing produce?

Some lift and some drag

In level flight what proportions of lift will be produced by the upper and lower surfaces of an aerofoil?

Upper - 2/3
Lower - 1/3

What is the Centre of Pressure?

The point on the aerofoil chord line through which the total aerodynamic force acts

What happens to the C of P as the angle of attack is increased to the stall?

It moves forward until it reaches its most forward point just before the stalling angle

What usually happens to the C of P and pitch when trailing edge flap is lowered?

The C of P moves aft (and the lateral C of P moves towards the wing root) causing a nose down pitching moment

What is the stalling angle?

The angle of attack above which the aerofoil stalls

When is lift at a maximum?

At the stalling angle

080 POF

PRINCIPLES OF FLIGHT

Where does lift act?

Lift acts at the C of P and in a direction perpendicular to the free stream air flow (or line of flight)

What happens to lift above the stalling angle?

Lift is still produced but not enough to support the aeroplane

What is induced drag proportional to?

$Lift^2$, $weight^2$, load $factor^2$, downwash, vortices

As speed is increased in level flight what happens to induced drag and why?

It reduces because the angle of attack is decreased as speed increases

How is induced drag related to speed?

Induced drag is inversely proportional to and reduces as the square of the speed $(1/V^2)$

How is profile drag related to speed?

Profile drag is proportional to and increases as the square of the speed (V^2)

What is Vmd?

Velocity minimum drag: The velocity at which induced drag equals profile drag

Where is induced drag the greatest?

At the wing tip where it originates

What is aspect ratio?

Span / Mean chord or $Span^2$ / Area

What is a high aspect ratio wing?

One with long span and short chord (e.g. a glider)

PRINCIPLES OF FLIGHT

What aspect ratio wing produces less induced drag?

A high aspect ratio wing (e.g. a glider has less induced drag)

What happens to air at the wing tip?

Air flows from the underside to the upper surface and down behind the trailing edge, therefore forming a vortex

How can control flutter be reduced?

Using a mass balance on the control surface

What happens to stalling angle when trailing edge flap is lowered?

It reduces stalling angle

What are Fowler flaps for?

They increase wing camber and wing area

What happens when the left rudder pedal is pushed forward with a balance tab assisted rudder?

The rudder trailing edge moves to port and the balance tab to the left yawing the aircraft to port

How is secondary roll produced?

With left rudder and left yaw, the right wing moves faster through the air producing more lift and therefore roll to port

How are the ailerons positioned in left roll?

Port aileron up
Starboard aileron down

How is adverse aileron yaw corrected?

With differential ailerons with the up going aileron travelling further
With the Frise aileron with the leading edge projecting into the airflow increasing profile drag

080 POF

PRINCIPLES OF FLIGHT

With respect to weight, drag, thrust, and lift - what is the angle of climb dependent on?

Excess of thrust over drag

With respect to weight, drag, thrust, (power), and lift - what is the rate of climb dependent on?

Excess of power

With respect to weight, drag, thrust, and lift - what happens in the glide?

Thrust is replaced by some weight

What does wind do to glide range?

Tailwind increases glide range
Headwind decreases glide range

In a power off glide what is the relationship between thrust and drag?

Drag is greater than thrust (thrust is zero)

In a glide what is the relationship between lift and weight?

Lift is less than weight

In a glide what are the forces acting on the aeroplane?

Lift, drag and weight

How is excessive lateral stability in swept wings reduced?

By using anhedral

How does aspect ratio affect induced drag?

An increase in aspect ratio reduces induced drag

PRINCIPLES OF FLIGHT

How may root stall be encouraged?

Wing twist so the tip has a smaller angle of incidence than the root
High camber at the tip
Stall inducer fitted at the root

How may lateral stability be increased?

By employing dihedral

What is a split flap?

A split flap is one where the top surface of the mainplane remains unbroken and the bottom rear surface moves downwards but not rearwards

What are the drag implications of split flaps?

Split flaps increase drag without increasing lift when moved from mid to fully down position.
Split flaps are only used for landing because of their large drag when fully lowered

What is the main reason for lowering flaps?

To slow down

In steady level flight what is thrust equal to?

Drag

How can aspect ratio be changed to reduce drag?

Increasing aspect ratio reduces induced drag
Decreasing aspect ratio reduces profile drag at high speeds

What happens to lift and drag when a wing stalls?

Lift decreases and drag increases

PRINCIPLES OF FLIGHT

What is profile drag is proportional to?

Shape and roughness
Size
TAS
Air density

If an aircraft accelerates in level flight what happens to the C of P?

It moves aft

What is thickness / chord ratio?

Maximum aerofoil thickness / chord length

What is wash in?

An increase in angle of incidence from root to tip (the opposite of wash out)

What is the formula for lift?

$L = C_L \frac{1}{2}\rho V^2 S$

What is the formula for drag?

$D = C_D \frac{1}{2}\rho V^2 S$

How is stalling speed affected by weight?

New V_S = Old V_S x $\sqrt{}$ (new weight / old weight)

What is the load factor in a turn?

Load factor = 1 / cosine (angle of bank)

How is stalling speed affected by load factor?

New V_S = Level flight V_S x $\sqrt{}$ (load factor)

How do slots delay the stall?

By delaying the onset of the smooth airflow break up

PRINCIPLES OF FLIGHT

How does stalling speed change with angle of bank?

New V_S = Old V_S x $\sqrt{}$ (cosine old angle of bank / cosine new angle of bank)

What affects rate of turn and radius of turn?

Speed and angle of bank (weight does not have an effect)

What are the three axes about which an aircraft is affected in flight?

Pitching about the lateral axis
Rolling about the longitudinal axis
Yawing about the normal axis

What must be done if an aircraft has been overstressed?

It must be inspected by a qualified engineer prior to its next flight.

What is the Lift / Weight nose down couple in level flight balanced by?

A downward force produced by the tailplane

What is the function of an anti-balance tab?

To increase stick loads as the control deflection increases.

Will the use of flap for take-off increase the climb out angle?

No, it degrades the climb out but gives a shorter take-off ground run

What gives an aircraft directional stability?

The fin

What is neutral stability?

When the aircraft remains in the new position after being disturbed from its trimmed position

COMMUNICATIONS

What does the abbreviation HJ mean?

Sunrise to sunset

How do you ask for a radio serviceability check?

"Request radio check"

What are the readability scales?

1 Unreadable
2 Readable now and then
3 Readable but with difficulty
4 Readable
5 Perfectly readable

When may an aircraft use an abbreviated call sign?

When it has been addressed in an abbreviated form by a ground station?

Can an aerodrome FIS provide instructions or control?

No only information

What is the correct abbreviation for Jetline G-JETC?

"Jetline TC"

How should a pilot correct an error in transmission?

Say: "Correction" then repeat the last correct word or phrase and then continue

How are numbers transmitted?

100   Wun hundred
583   Fife ait tree
11000 Wun Wun tousand
25000 Two fife tousand

How is time 0947 transmitted?

"Four seven" or "zero nine four seven"

COMMUNICATIONS

₂ What does STANDBY mean? 3 7

Wait to be called

What does AFFIRM mean? 3 7

Yes or In agreement

What does ROGER mean? 3 7

Last message has been received

What is the order of priority of radiotelephony message?

Distress
Urgency
Direction Finding
Flight safety
Meteorological
Flight regularity

What is DISTRESS?

A condition of being threatened by serious and / or imminent danger and or requiring immediate assistance.

What is URGENCY?

A condition concerning the safety of an aircraft or other vehicle or some person on board or within sight but which does not require immediate assistance

How would a ground station providing Approach services be addressed?

"... Approach"

How would a ground station providing direction finding services be addressed?

"... Homer"

090 COM

COMMUNICATIONS

How would a ground station providing air / ground services be addressed?

"......Radio"

How do you 'Transmit Blind'?

Make your radiotelephony call, followed by "TRANSMITTING BLIND" and then the time of next intended message

What is the correct procedure to follow when encountering two-way radio failure when flying VMC?

Continue to fly VMC and land at the nearest suitable airfield

What is the correct procedure to follow when encountering two-way radio failure when flying IMC?

Proceed as per filed flight plan to designated navigational aid of destination aerodrome and hold until commencement of descent

What is the aeronautical mobile service?

A radio communication service between aircraft stations and aeronautical stations, or between aircraft stations

What is an aeronautical station?

A station in the aeronautical mobile service located on land or at sea

What is a Radar Information Service RIS?

Information on conflicting traffic will be given but no avoiding action

On initial contact to an ATSU what should the message include?

Call sign and service requested

With which air traffic service would you file an airborne flight plan?

FIS

090 COM

COMMUNICATIONS

What is the international distress frequency?

121.5 MHz

When ATC asks if you can maintain 120 KT your reply should be?

"Affirm" or "negative"

Who can impose radio silence in a distress situation?

The aircraft in distress or the station in control

When is a Special VFR (SVFR) clearance issued?

To allow flights in control zones at the request of the pilot

What is the range of communications frequencies in the VHF band?

118 to 136.975 MHz

In speechless code what is SAY AGAIN?

Three short transmissions

What clearances must be read back relating to the runway in use?

Clearances to enter, land on, take-off from, cross and back track the runway in use

When are the words "TAKE OFF" used? 2 3

Only when an aircraft is cleared for take-off or cancelling a take-off clearance

Give an example of a conditional clearance?

"G-BKEY after the landing Cessna line up"

How should you indicate that you are ready for take-off?

"Ready for departure"

090 COM

COMMUNICATIONS

What phrase is used to indicate that a take-off has been abandoned?

"STOPPING"

How is time transmitted?

Normally the minutes of the hour are transmitted, the hour should be included if there is a possibility of confusion
UTC must be used

What is QDM?

Magnetic track to a station

What is QDR?

Magnetic bearing of an aircraft from a station

What is the accuracy of a class B bearing?

±5°

When is it allowable for controllers to transmit to aircraft during take-off, last part of final approach or the landing roll?

In the interest of safety

What is considered a long final?

On final approach between 8 NM and 4 NM from the threshold

At an airfield providing flight information when given 'Land at your discretion' how should the pilot respond?

"G-BKEY" or "landing G-BKEY"

On which frequency should a mayday call be transmitted if already in contact with an ATSU?

The current frequency in use

090 COM

COMMUNICATIONS

How may IFR departure instructions be given?

In plain language or as a SID (Standard Instrument Departure)

What are the two parts of a call sign of an aeronautical station?

Name of the location followed by the suffix (e.g. Control, Approach)

What are the elements of a position report?

Aircraft identification
Position
Time
Level
Next position and ETA

What is the call sign for approach control?

"… Approach"

When may you abbreviate call sign to suffix only?

After being addressed in this manner by the aeronautical station

When is the word "HEAVY" used?

By aircraft in the heavy wake turbulence category immediately after the call sign in the initial call

What is ATIS?

Automatic Terminal Information Service

When would you change your call sign in flight?

When instructed to by an air traffic control unit

What is the requirement to read back ATC route clearances?

Must always be read back unless otherwise authorised

090 COM

COMMUNICATIONS

What is the requirement to read back other clearances including conditional clearances?

Should be read back or acknowledged in a manner that indicates they have been understood and accepted

What is the requirement to read back runway in use, SSR codes, level instructions, etc?

They must always be read back

How should you refer to vertical position?

FL   - Standard Pressure Setting
Altitude - QNH
Height - QFE

What action should be taken by a station which receives a distress message?

Immediately acknowledge distress message
Take control of communications (or transfer that responsibility)
Inform ATS unit concerned

What action should be taken by a station which receives a urgency message?

Acknowledge urgency message
Inform ATS unit concerned
Take control of communications if necessary

When requesting a MATZ penetration what is the latest distance / time for the request to be made?

15 NM / 5 min

Squawk mode charlie means what?

Turn on altitude reporting (mode C) on the transponder

When referring to climbs and descents to a height or altitude should the word 'to' be used?

Yes, but not when referring to flight levels

090 COM

COMMUNICATIONS

When making a standard overhead join to a circuit what is the first descending call?

"G-BKEY deadside descending"

When requesting MATZ penetration what information should be given?

Call sign, type, position, heading, altitude / FL, intentions

When transmitting an urgency call what does the prefix 'tyro' indicate?

The low experience level of the pilot

How should the decimal point in frequencies be pronounced?

Day-see-mal

What does the phrase "go around" mean?

Execute a missed approach

What is the correct sequence of a distress (Mayday) message?

Mayday x 3
Name of station being addressed
Identification of the aircraft
Nature of distress condition
Intention of pilot-in-command
Present position, level and heading

What is the correct sequence of an urgency (Pan Pan) message?

Pan Pan x 3
Name of station being addressed
Identification of aircraft
Nature of urgency condition
Intention of pilot-in-command
Present position, level and heading

What does the term "UNDER RADAR CONTROL" mean?

Radar control service is being provided

090 COM

COMMUNICATIONS

What does the term SQUAWK IDENT mean?

Operate the transponder IDENT feature

What is the transponder code for unlawful interference (hijack)?

7500

What is the transponder code for radio failure?

7600

What is the transponder code for emergency?

7700

What does RVR mean?

Runway visual range

When should aircraft routine meteorological observations be made?

At routine position reporting points or distances corresponding to approximately one hour's flying time

When should a special observation (SPECI) be made?

When encountering conditions which may affect safety and efficiency of aircraft operations such as: severe turbulence or icing, volcanic ash cloud

and additionally moderate turbulence, hail or cumulonimbus for transonic / supersonic flight

When can SAFETYCOM transmissions be made?

Within 2000' aal, 1000' above circuit height, within 10 NM of aerodrome

What is the purpose of the prefix STUDENT?

To alert controllers and other airspace users to the presence of student pilots flying solo

090 COM

LIST OF ABBREVIATIONS

'	feet	MNPS	Minimum Navigation Performance Specification
ADF	Automatic Direction Finder	MSA	Minimum Safe Altitude
AGL	Above Ground Level	NDB	Non-Directional Beacon
AH	Artificial Horizon	NM	nautical mile(s)
AIP	Aeronautical Information Publication	OAT	Outside Air Temperature
ALT	Altimeter	OBS	Omni Bearing Selector
ANT	Antenna switch	OIS	Obstacle Identification Surface
APP	Approach	O/H	Overhead
ASI	Air Speed Indicator	OTS	Organised Track System
ATC	Air Traffic Control	PFL	Practice Forced Landing
ATIS	Automated Terminal Information System	POSN	Position
		QDM	Magnetic bearing TO
BCARs	British Civil Airworthiness Requirements	QDR	Magnetic bearing FROM
BKN	Broken (5-7 oktas)	QFE	Pressure in hPa such that altimeter reads zero feet at aerodrome level
CAA	Civil Aviation Authority		
CMR	Certificate of Maintenance Review	QNH	Pressure in hPa such that altimeter reads airfield elevation above mean sea level
CPL	Commercial Pilot's Licence		
CPL(A)	Commercial Pilot's Licence (Aeroplanes)		
CRS	Certificate of Release to Service	RT	Radiotelephony
CTZ	Control Zone	RAS	Radar Advisory Service
DI	Direction Indicator	RFIX	Radio Fix
DIST	Distance	RIS	Radar Information Service
DMAX	Maximum Drift	RMI	Radio Magnetic Indicator
DME	Distance Measuring Equipment	RVR	Runway Visual Range
EASA	European Aviation Safety Agency	s	second(s)
EFATO	Engine Failure After Take Off	SFC	Surface
eta	estimated time of arrival	TAS	True Air Speed
FCL	Flight Crew Licensing	TC	Turn Co-ordinator
FE	Flight Examiner	TDZ	Touch Down Zone
FIS	Flight Information Service	TRK	Track
FNPT II	Flight and Navigation Procedures Trainer II	TW	Tailwind
		TWR	Tower
FL	Flight Level	Ts and Ps	Temperatures and Pressures
'	feet	V_A	Velocity for Approach
GRND	Ground	V_{AT}	Velocity for Approach at Threshold
GS	Ground Speed		
G/S	Glide Slope	V_{NE}	Velocity Never Exceed
h	hour(s)	V_R	Velocity for Rotation
HDG	Heading	V_x	Velocity for maximum angle of climb
hPa	Hectopascal(s)		
HSI	Horizontal Situation Indicator	V_y	Velocity for maximum rate of climb
HW	Headwind	VAR	Variation
IAS	Indicated Air Speed	VDF	Very high frequency Direction Finding
ICAO	International Civil Aviation Organisation		
		VFR	Visual Flight Rules
IEM	Interpretive & Explanatory Material	VSI	Vertical Speed Indicator
IF	Instrument Flight	VOR	Very high frequency Omni-directional Range finding (beacon)
IFR	Instrument Flight Rules		
IMC	Instrument Meteorological Conditions	W/V	Wind Velocity
INFO	Information		
km	kilometre(s)		
LAMS	Light Aircraft Maintenance Document		
LARS	Lower Airspace Radar Service		
m	metre(s)		
MATZ	Military Aerodrome Traffic Zone		
min	minute(s)		

LIST OF USEFUL CONTACTS

Authorities

U.K. Civil Aviation Authority
Flight Crew Licensing
Aviation House
Gatwick Airport South
West Sussex RH6 07R
www.caa.co.uk

Schools

For a list of current Approved Training
Organisations see:
www.caa.co.uk

List of Suppliers

Pooleys Flight Equipment Limited
Elstree Aerodrome
Hertfordshire WD6 3AW
Tel: 0208 953 4870

Transair (U.K.) Limited
Shoreham Airport
Shoreham-by-Sea
West Sussex, England
BN43 5PA
Tel: 01273 466 000

Free PPL theory course details

www.catsppl.com